People Who Read

Notable People

"Is this book worth it? Just using one of the techniques that Steven described has saved my wife and me almost $57,000 in college expenses – and that is just on one kid."

– Charles Dobens, Founder, Multifamily Investing Academy

"This book should be required for anyone going to college. It is invaluable information that all students need to know prior to enrolling."

– Paul Ray, Utah House of Representatives

"This fast-moving, practical book is loaded with proven strategies to lower college costs, get an excellent education, and graduate debt-free. Wow!"

– Brian Tracy, Author, Goals!

"I couldn't put it down. Little did I know what an amazing experience I was in for! I am just blown away by the power of that book! It was absolutely eye-opening to me - I'm so glad I got to read it!! It's not only a must-read for college students, but for EVERYONE!!!!!"

– Christy Ray, TPR Story Telling, Blaine Ray Workshops.

Students and Graduates

"This is the best 'How-To' book I have ever read about college. Very well done."

– John Paul Cutler, Student

"I really like this book! I would give it an 'A.' It is very helpful and there are a lot of ideas that I have never heard about or considered before…. If you know someone going to college, I recommend you get this book."

– Christina LeBaron, Student

"Who knew that a book on saving money could be so fun to read? Awesome job!"

– Justin Swalberg, MBA

"This book is entertaining while you learn what's needed. It was really nice to see it all in a kind of simulated situation besides just the abstract. I couldn't wait to finish it because I wanted to see how the main character was able to solve his financial problems. It's a story that's fun to read, but I was also learning while reading the story – and enjoying it."

– Tiffany Marvin-Carr, Student

"This book takes the informative format and puts it into an interesting adventure through its storytelling. The narrative includes the educational content embedded within – and the author combines the two quite seamlessly. It's almost as if a reader could learn the ideas in the book without realizing that they were having them taught to them, but instead through absorption of the story."

– Keaton Charles Butler, Student Writer

"I was worried this would be an instructive book and that I would get bored while reading. This was not the case because the storyline implements all of the principles in an interesting and intriguing way. The way things are presented in the book help me to learn – both things to do and what to avoid. I really liked the concept of the *Bubblegum-Diamond-Thief* and *money management*. I recommend this book to my friends – I think it's excellent for people both in and outside of college."

– Ashley Rees, Student

"A compelling read that made me wish I had this book before I went to school – back when I was young and stupid. I could have saved myself a lot of money and years of paying back debt. I recommend this book to anyone."

– Emily Grover, College Graduate

Topics and Principles Taught in the Book

- Scholarship sequencing
- Scholarship essay writing
- Scholarship stacking
- Tuition reimbursement
- Avoiding credit card debt
- Getting dreams
- Internship tips
- Consequences of debt
- Avoiding student loans
- Short term loans
- Service and giving back
- Tax management
- Automatic bill payment
- Fixed and fluctuating expenses
- 529 Education Savings Plans
- Money maximization
- Importance of study groups
- Jobs that act like scholarships
- How to get good credit cards
- Systematizing applications
- School financial counselors
- FAFSA
- Book buying
- 401(k) plans
- Money seeds
- Saving money
- Getting deals
- Goal setting
- Net worth
- Essay citing
- BillPay
- Freedom fund
- Money priorities

WINNING THE MONEY GAME
In College, BOOK 1: FINANCE

Any Major and Any GPA Can Finish College Debt Free or Better!

Steven C. Roberts

www.CollegeCashChampion.com

Rosebud Publications • Clearfield, UT

WINNING THE MONEY GAME *In College,*
BOOK 1: FINANCE

Any Major and Any GPA Can Finish College Debt Free or Better!

Rosebud Publications
98 N Main ST #222
Clearfield, UT 84015

Editions Available – First Edition 2014   10 9 8 7 6 5 4 3 2 1

| Paperback | 978-0-9903147-0-7 | PDF | 978-0-9903147-1-4 |
| Mobipocket | 978-0-9903147-2-1 | EPUB | 978-0-9903147-3-8 |

Library of Congress Control Number: 2014909327

Foreword

The moment your first child is born, you begin to hear the almost daily mantra from other parents, 'eighteen more years before you have to start writing big checks', 'I hope she is a great athlete' or my favorite 'have you started a college fund yet?' This last one is usually from a stockbroker or insurance agent trying to sell you something.

Here's one thought before you decide to sign on the dotted line and take out student loans for yourself or for your kids; student loans cannot be discharged in bankruptcy. Think about that for a moment. The federal government has made a deal with the issuers of student loans such that if the borrower gets into financial trouble, their mortgage may be discharged along with everything else, except, the student loans. The student loans take priority over most other forms of debt and cannot be dismissed – or even in many cases, the loan cannot be paid off early even if you have the money to do so. Those student loan companies must have great lobbyists.

So, before you start 'mortgaging' your future in the form of student loans, let's shift your paradigm. That is what this book is designed to do. Think outside the box. Change your perspective. Think differently than what Madison Avenue is teaching you.

In this book, my friend Steven Roberts will take you on a journey. For some people, it will be a historical narrative and for others it will change your life and put you on a path to financial freedom the likes that many never know but is available to all. While the book is fictional in terms of the characters, the principles are true. What many people don't know about the book is that many of the principles and events, Steven actually lived and practiced. He knows from firsthand experience that it is possible to pay for college without taking out student loans or hitting mom and dad up for money.

My wife and I have begun implementing many of the techniques that Steven lays out in this book. It is such a great feeling when you see the total cost of your child's college experience comes nowhere close to the 'retail' price that is advertised in the manuals found in every bookstore.

Is this book worth it? Just using one of the techniques that Steven described has saved my wife and me almost $57,000 in college expenses – and that is just on one kid. I have three more to go. If you can have that type of success as easily as we have, the answer is an emphatic, yes, this book is worth GOLD.

Charles Dobens,
Boston, MA

How to Use This Book

This is not a standard finance book – it is a story to teach principles. My hope is that you will enjoy reading this book and use the principles as you can see them implemented by the characters' interactions. *Winning the Money Game in College* is a story and an instructional guide. The book will read like a novel – you will follow Justin, a college freshman who learns two days before classes that he is completely on his own; the principles are interwoven in the story. At the end of each chapter the principles are outlined as tips and suggestions, along with warnings and things to avoid.

As a suggestion, read through the story first. Other readers have said that the story greatly helps them understand both what to do and how to implement the suggestions. After reading the story, you can either read through the end of chapter material and/or continue reading the next chapter. Reading the material may help to solidify the suggestions contained in the chapter. Also, the end of chapter material will allow you to quickly reference the suggestions contained in the chapter. This reference can be used now and later.

While many of the suggestions and ideas may seem specific to a certain location, please do an internet search with your state, or location, for that specific service (i.e. "Michigan 529 Education Savings Plan" instead of the "Utah 529 Education Savings Plan or UESP" mentioned in the book). I had to pick a location, so I picked my state, but know that the principles taught in the story can be applied generally to most places in the United States.

For quick reference, use the Table of Contents to look up the principles and then read the specific section or end of chapter material. Most of all, enjoy the book. It is written to engage both the right and left brain as you will learn by reading the story and the practical advice that the story contains. You may soon forget you are reading a book on money and finance and simply enjoy the story.

This book is dedicated to Jana – my love and sweetheart.
Jana my love, thank you for all of your support and encouragement – not just with this book, but always.

I love you.

Contents

Chapter 1: A Rude Awakening

"What do you mean Dad can't keep his promise?" a surprised Justin asked his mom on the phone.

"I know that this is hard to hear," his mom replied through the phone, "but we are no longer going to be able to pay for your college expenses like we said we would."

"What happened? I mean when I left home yesterday, Dad reassured me that he would pay for my schooling and I didn't need to worry. What changed? Is Dad hurt?"

"Dad is fine physically, but this morning about 9 o'clock our time, while you were at Grandma and Grandpa's house, Dad's work gave him the option of either taking a 60% reduction in pay or be laid off. Dad said that management presented the company losses and he chose to have a pay cut. He came home early and told me. We're cutting every expense we can, and right now we simply can't meet other financial obligations and pay for your schooling."

"What are you going to do?" Justin asked, hoping that there was another solution to the problem.

"Dad is putting his résumé together and will stay on while he looks for a new job. I am sorry, Honey, but we need to look out for our family and your siblings here. We are not going to be able to help you with your schooling costs."

The news hit Justin as if he were being run over by a truck. This was really hard to take. Justin was not prepared for what his mom had said. A strong sinking feeling settled in his stomach. He hadn't planned on this and the news just made him feel sick.

Justin had left home in Bakersfield, California, the previous day to attend Syracuse State University[1] in Utah. Before he left, his dad reiterated the promise of paying for Justin's schooling. After staying with his grandparents in Saint George, Utah, to break up the trip, Justin had gotten a flat tire. He was now stuck at the side of the freeway with a flat tire, about a mile before the off-ramp for Springfield, Utah. Even without the flat tire, he was about 3 hours away from his final destination. The tire would only delay him further.

Hoping that perhaps he could ask for an "advance" for some of the money that his dad was going to pay for school to help with the tire, Justin called his mom. That was when he received the bad news: "We are not going to be able to keep our promise to pay for your college."

"What am I going to do? School starts in two days and if I don't get my prerequisites finished this semester, I won't be accepted for my major," Justin asked, pleading for a solution.

"Justin," his mom responded in a tone that only mothers can give. "You're 21 years old; you've been away from home before when you worked in Alaska as a tour guide bus driver and on a humanitarian service project in Ecuador. You were able to provide for yourself in both of those times in your life. You'll have to figure this out, too."

As his mother paused on the phone, Justin was remembering what his grandpa had told him while he was at his house. As Justin was going for a run, he found his grandpa reading, and his Grandpa read aloud:

"'For which of you, intending to build a tower, sitteth not down first, and counteth the cost, whether he have sufficient to finish it?'"[2] Justin's grandpa then added, "Many of the world's problems come from disregarding these two principles: taking a proper accounting of your money and living within your means."

"Most of Christ's parables were about money. In fact, Christ instructed us to learn about money.[3] You're at an important time in your life, Justin. Learn everything you can about money and how

---

1 Fictitious school used at the time of writing.

2 Luke 14:28, King James Version

3 See Luke 16:9, KJV

it works. The habits you establish now will go with you for the rest of your life..."

Justin now felt a heavy burden as he realized that he was completely unprepared for being able to pay for college, and felt that Grandpa's advice was only condemning him for a lack of preparation. At the time, it felt like sage advice from an old man that Justin would soon forget, but now as he was speaking with his mom, he felt bitter towards the situation and his dad's company. However, out of his mouth, Justin heard himself say:

"It'll be fine, Mom. I can find a way. I'll get a student loan or something."

"Be prayerful and make wise decisions, Honey. We will be praying for you."

"Thanks, Mom," Justin said, knowing that bringing up his flat tire again to ask for any money was out of the question.

"You might want to call Dave and Susan and tell them that you are going to be late," Justin's mother reminded him.

Before leaving Bakersfield, Justin's older cousin Dave and his wife Susan had agreed to let Justin stay at their home a few miles from the university for one week or until Justin found a place to stay—whichever came first.

"'Kay, I'll give them a call."

"Wherever you go to get your tire fixed ask them if they have any discounts for college students—remember to get the price first, and then ask for the discount in order to prevent being bid up by the people who fix your tire."

"Thanks," Justin said half-heartedly. He said his good-byes and went to work on changing the tire.

For a long time, Justin's dad had promised to pay for schooling, and with his departure yesterday, Justin had felt that his life was just about perfect. With acceptance to SSU, Justin being able to take the prerequisites offered in fall semester, his dad paying for schooling costs, and living at his cousin's house for a week, Justin thought *I've got it made.*

What sealed the deal for going to SSU was when Justin found out his good friend Paul was already there. Paul and Justin had made plans to hang out—starting with going to a dance together two days before classes were to begin. Now two days before classes started, Justin was at the side of the freeway trying to change a flat tire; the dance was supposed to start in four hours, and Justin had no idea how to pay for school.

Moment of Decision and Taking Action

Justin called his cousin Dave, but only got his voicemail. He left a message about the tire and said he would call back. Justin started to change his tire, his mind racing with options of what he was going to do to pay for school. *If I don't start this semester, I won't get my pre-req's done and I won't be able to be accepted into my major. I don't care how… I am going to still go to school. I will find a way. I want to be accepted by my major. I have got about $1,000 in my bank account, maybe I can get a student loan for the rest. Perhaps I can meet with a representative from a bank. Why did Dad's work have to go and do a thing like that? I guess, I will just do what everyone else does, I mean, I can always pay it off after I graduate, right? What am I going to do? How do I tell Paul I am going to be late? He's waiting for me at SSU.*

Once the spare was in place, he pulled out his phone again. This time he searched for a tire store; an app gave him directions, and he was soon on his way to buy a new tire.

Asking for a Discount

Upon entering the store, Justin announced to a store clerk: "I have a flat tire. What would it cost to get it replaced including parts, labor, and all fees, as the final cost?" After getting some vehicle information, the clerk gave him a quote.

Justin then asked: "Do you have any specials or discounts for students?" Justin was remembering the conversation with his mom, and knew that he needed every penny to pay for school.

"We do have a discount for students, offering 10% off," replied the man. "Do you have your student ID?"

"I am a freshman, my car is packed and I am headed up to Syracuse State University; I don't have a student ID yet."

After a bit of consideration, the salesman replied, "I'd be willing to give you 10% off without your ID."

"That sounds great," Justin said, disgruntled about the flat tire but happy to get a discount.

"There's a bit of a wait, so we won't be able to get to this for another thirty to forty minutes. People always seem to wait till the close of the day to come in," warned the clerk.

"Good to know. After the wait, how long will it take to change the tire?" Justin asked hopefully.

"About thirty minutes."

Justin figured that there was no guarantee that if he went to a new store, that he would get a discount. Additionally, considering how close it was to closing time, he might not even get serviced today.

"Well, let's get started," Justin said. "My car is the green Toyota Tercel." He handed the clerk his keys.

He took a seat in the waiting area. His mind went back and forth to how he was going to pay for school. While Justin was waiting, he decided to call his cousin. Dave's phone rang three times, and just as Justin thought he would have to leave a voicemail again, he heard a hurried "Hello!" from the phone.

"Hi, Dave, this is Justin."

"Hey, how's it going?" asked his older cousin. "I got your message. Were you able to get your tire taken care of?"

"Well, I was able to get the spare put on, and I'm at a tire store now. The clerk said that it would take over an hour, due to the last-minute rush," Justin responded.

"That should put you here about 8:30 to 9:00, assuming all goes well, right?" asked Dave. After agreeing, his cousin added, "Well, be safe. When you get here, I'll help you unload and show you where you can sleep."

"Okay, thanks," said Justin. "Hey Dave…" Justin began.

"Yeah"

"How'd you pay for school? I mean I was just wondering how to make ends meet," Justin said, not wanting to mention his dad's pay cut to his cousin.

"Well, I was able to get a student loan and that saw me through school. If you need to, you can meet with a school student counselor that specializes in student loans. College can be rough financially, but it may help you get a higher income."

"Thanks for the info," Justin said.

They said their good-byes and hung up their phones. Justin was deflated by his cousin's words, but also because of the time.

It'll be 9 p.m. when I get there? I don't know if I'm going to make it to this dance, Justin thought. *I'd better call Paul.*

"Justin! Are you in Syracuse?" asked Paul excitedly as he answered the phone.

"Well, actually, my car had a flat tire. Now I'm in a tire store in a small town called Springville."

Paul responded, "That's about three hours away. How are you planning on making it to the dance?"

"Um, *I* was wondering that, as well," Justin said in a slightly disappointed tone. It wasn't so much the dance that he was interested in—it was seeing Paul again. "The tire guy said that it would be just under an hour before my car would be finished," continued Justin.

"Yeah, I guess… but maybe we can do *something* when you get in," said Paul. "The dance goes until 10:00."

"I'll call you when I get to Syracuse, but don't count on it being early enough to do go the dance," replied Justin.

"Well, that's no fun," Paul pouted jokingly. "Take care, though. Oh– and don't rush it; I-15 has a couple speed traps. I wouldn't push it too much. With California plates, your car kind of sticks out like a sore thumb," said Paul.

"Thanks for the warning," said Justin.

"Don't worry," continued Paul. "This dance isn't the only thing to do at SSU. We'll still have plenty of time to hang out and do stuff together."

Justin wondered if he should tell Paul about his dad's employment and his sudden lack of funds—this would severely limit his fun.

"Hey, do you know how to get a student loan?" Justin asked, trying not to sound too obvious or desperate.

"Wait, why do you care? Isn't your dad going to pay for your college anyway? Student loans are for the rest of us who don't have it made," Paul said with a hint of curiosity.

"Dad's work had him take a 60% pay cut instead of a layoff. Now my parents can't afford to pay for my school."

"*Ewllll*... Dude, that stinks!" Paul said.

"Tell me about it." Justin replied. "I am still coming to school, but now I need to come up with funds soon."

"We can make it happen; you can get a student loan and maybe I might be able to help you learn some ways to save some money." Paul said. "We can still have a lot of fun together when you get up here."

"We'd better," said Justin jokingly. "Take care."

"See ya' man," Paul replied, in a friendly tone.

Justin soon regretted not grabbing some of his food from the assortment of snacks his grandma had put together. He looked around the store for vending machines and in the corner saw some small candy dispensers that had chalky chocolate candies in them. Justin looked out the window of the tire store and saw a fast-food joint. He thought about going there and grabbing something to eat.

Hmmm, a couple of tacos and some enchiladas, he thought. *This could be good.* He walked towards the front of the tire store. But then he realized that he didn't want to blow any money when he already had food available—especially now that he was paying for school. He went back to the same man who had helped him when he came into the store.

"It will be about another ten minutes before we get to your car," the man said before Justin could say anything.

"Thanks," Justin said, as friendly as he could be considering the long wait ahead. "I just wanted to have my keys so that I could get some food from my car."

"Sure thing," replied the man as he grabbed Justin's keys and then tossed them to him. "Just have the keys back soon so I can get them to the mechanic."

"Thanks," said Justin. He went out and unlocked his car door. After rummaging through his care package from his grandma, he grabbed some fruit and crackers and a water bottle. He re-locked his car and knocked on the door of the store to be let back inside. He handed the keys back to the man.

Sitting down again, Justin started fiddling with his Smartphone. After eating more of his quick meal, he felt significantly better.

Eventually the clerk came to him and said, "Your car's ready to go. I can ring you up at the register." Justin followed the man over to the register and was given his invoice. "Your total is $76.73," said the man. Justin paid and soon enough he was back on the road.

The rest of the trip passed without incident. Justin arrived in Syracuse a little after 9:20 p.m. and drove to Dave's. Justin was welcomed in and shown where he could sleep. He brought some of his bags in and by this time it was after 10:15. Justin called Paul and said he didn't feel up to getting together this late. He was disappointed, but Paul understood. Justin got ready for bed. He was tired after traveling all day and fell right to sleep.

Chapter 1: Principles and Suggestions

Justin's Grandpa Jackson was correct: most financial problems occur when people don't take an accounting of their finances and live within their means. What are some ways to live within your means?

Find ways to save money. Learn to make your hard-earned dollars stretch farther. Be creative. Expect and find ways to get discounts. Here are some suggestions:

1. Make the decision to obtain your goals in spite of obstacles.

2. If you have a Smartphone, go to the App Store for Android, iPhone, Windows, or any other provider, and search for apps in the following categories:

    a. Grocery stores

    b. Gas stations

    c. Coupon finders

    d. Shopping lists that can automatically find the items at a discount for your area—saving both time and money

        Look for generic apps that have high user ratings and over 1,000 downloads. You want apps that are secure and do not have access to your personal information.

3. Have money set aside for emergencies. Every month save at least 5 to 10% in an account that you don't touch. Save this way until you have at least $300 to $500. Remember, this is an emergency fund—it is to only be used in an emergency. Buying groceries or going to a restaurant are not emergencies; tuition is not an emergency (with few exceptions); and no form of entertainment is an emergency. The following are examples of emergencies: when you are between jobs, when you have unexpected costs (i.e., sickness), or when you would be unable to attend a particular semester of school due to a lack of funds,and you have exhausted other means.

4. Automate your expenses by having apps for your Smartphone that will help you plan. (As an alternative, see the chapters on automatic saving and spending.)

5. Be sure to ask for the final quote before asking for deals. Many times merchants *say that they w*ill give you a discount, but then charge fees to that eliminate your savings.

6. Ask for and expect discounts. Ask for businesses to honor competitors' coupons. You won't always get it, but by asking, you can at least find out if they will offer a discount. Many businesses will offer student discounts and/or honor competitor coupons to get your business. The worst that could happen is they'll say no.

7. What checks can you provide yourself so that you stay on your plan? If you find yourself with a desire to spend, here are some suggestions:

   a. Carry prepaid-debit that are PIN accessible instead of ordinary credit cards.

   b. Familiarize yourself with your plan so that you know your pre-determined limits.

   c. Use the automatic savings and automatic spending tips in Chapters 7-12.

   d. Review your purchases so that you know how much you have available in each category.

Chapter 1: Warnings and Avoidance

1. Have you ever spent money that you later regretted? What caused you to purchase what you did? What might have helped prevent your spending that money? How does Will Roger's lesson apply to you? He's quoted as saying: "Too many people spend money they haven't earned to buy things they don't want, to impress people they don't like."[4]

2. Justin stopped himself from buying unneeded restaurant food. How could you avoid spending money, a little here and a little there? This is what is referred to as the *Bubblegum-Diamond-Thief*: trading small insignificant expenses for what you really want. It will be explained more in later chapters.

---

4 Will Rogers, Online, *http://www.wisebread.com/64-funny-inspiring-and-stupid-money-quotes-from-famous-people* . Available August 13, 2013.

Chapter 2: Decisions

After he got up the next morning and had his morning run, Justin hit the kitchen for breakfast. Dave came in, looking a little sleepy. "How's it going?" he asked as he rubbed his eyes briefly. "I have to get to work, but I would recommend, Justin, that you head over to the campus and try to see if you can find a job and get your student ID. I hear jobs on campus and in surrounding areas go quickly."

"Thanks," said Justin. "I was going to go get my student ID then look for a job. I have an appointment at 1 p.m. to see a school counselor for classes," he added.

"A counselor for *classes*?" Dave asked inquisitively.

"That's right," replied Justin.

"Man, you are brave," said Dave. "When I was a student there, by the day before classes started, all of the fun classes were gone."

"*Fun* classes?" Justin asked.

"Yeah, you know: the ones that make college bearable—things like volleyball, golf, and karate," said Dave.

"I guess I was focusing too much on the classes for my major," Justin responded. "I hadn't really thought about adding any *fun* classes to my schedule."

"Well, you'd better," emphasized Dave. "Oh, any luck with getting a student loan?"

"I will try to get an appointment later today."

"Well, good luck."

"Thanks," Justin said as he started to feel a little overwhelmed with all he had to do.

Justin, Dave, and Susan ate and then separated to get ready for their own activities for the day. Justin left to go to the Syracuse State University campus. When he arrived, he asked around and found out where the Student Center Building was. As he walked to it, he observed how beautiful the campus was, with its trees and landscaping. The buildings were similar to each other in design and had the same style of bricks. In addition to being well kept, the campus was also very busy: students and faculty members were making last-minute preparations for school the next day.

As Justin drew near to the Student Center, he noticed the building was already crowded with people busily moving around. He made his way to the front desk.

"I'm new here. Where do I go to get my student ID?" Justin asked a girl who stood behind the counter.

"Go down this hall and make a left. The ID Center is the second door on the right after you make the turn," the girl replied on semi-automatic pilot.

Justin thanked her and went on his way towards the ID Center. As Justin turned the corner, he saw a line extending out of the second door turning to the right.

In spite of what seemed like 30 people in front of him, the line moved quickly, and in less than 15 minutes, Justin was at the counter of one of the Center's staff members. After his photo was taken he was handed his student ID.

As he left the ID Center, his phone rang. It was Paul. Justin stepped away from the crowd to take the call.

"We missed you last night, man," were Paul's first words when Justin answered his phone.

"I know. Getting a flat tire on a trip has got to be on the list of 'Least Favorite Traveling Experiences,'" Justin replied.

"So where *are* you?"

"I'm in the Student Center. I just got my student ID and thought I would go buy some textbooks at the bookstore," Justin said.

"You're on campus! Sweet! So am I," was the reply. "Before you go to the bookstore, I have to show you something. Promise me you'll come meet me at the library. It will be well worth it to you *financially*, I mean," Paul said with emphasis.

"Okay. Where is the library?" Justin asked, absolutely lost already.

"It's the building to the south of the Student Center. I'll meet you in the library lobby," replied Paul.

"Okay, I should be there in a few minutes," Justin said as he started walking towards the library.

Justin had met Paul while on his humanitarian service project in Ecuador. They were both from California and had hit it off. Paul was a few months older than Justin and had been in Ecuador longer, so he had helped Justin to learn some of the more vital phrases in Spanish: *¿A qué hora viene el autobús?* (When does the bus come?), *¿Dondé está el baño?* (Where's the bathroom?), and *¡¿Qué pasa, calabaza?!* (What's happening? Literally: What's going on, pumpkin/pumpkin head?)

Paul had also been the source of some discomfort during Justin's first few weeks in Ecuador. The local women would occasionally provide meals for the volunteers, and Paul had told Justin that it was offensive to say "no" to more food. He had said that the polite way to decline additional helpings was to say *"Cómo no"* when offered more food. It wasn't until after his fourth helping of *sopa de pollo y arroz* (chicken and rice soup) that Justin had realized that it was a setup: *¿Cómo no?* means "Sure, why not?" Paul had thought his joke was hilarious, as Justin grabbed his bowl and covered it to prevent himself from gaining fifths on the dinner that night.

"Dude!" said Paul in the library lobby upon seeing Justin again.

"Hey, old man!" said Justin with a smile.

"Good to see ya', man," Paul said warmly.

"It's good to see *you*," said Justin as he gave Paul a quick hug.

"As you can see," said Paul, "the library is packed."

And it was. Justin had noticed people sitting at nearly every computer in the library's computer terminal section.

"This library has *talking* and *quiet* sections," Paul continued. "When I heard you were on campus, I grabbed us two computers in the talking section. We need to get back there soon so that someone doesn't move my stuff," Paul said, pointing to the area.

They walked quickly to the section Paul had indicated. On their way, Paul asked, "Did you have a good drive—minus the flat tire, I mean?"

"Yeah," replied Justin. "I was able to see my grandparents on my mom's side."

Paul suddenly stopped at a large desk with a sign that read "Computer Help" on it.

"You have your student ID, right?"

"Just got it!" replied Justin with enthusiasm because he realized he was an official student now.

"Excuse me," said Paul, turning to the attendant who was sitting at a computer, reading a book. The attendant looked up, so Paul continued speaking. "My friend here is a freshman on campus and would like to have access to the computer network."

"May I see your student ID?" the guy asked quickly. .

"Yeah," said Justin, supplying it to the attendant.

The attendant swiped the ID card and handed it back; he asked Justin what he wanted his username to be. After typing some other identifiable information into the computer, the attendant passed Justin the computer keyboard and asked him to type in a password. Justin did so and then returned the keyboard to the attendant.

"This is some job you've got here," Paul said.

"I know," said the attendant. "That should do it," he said to Justin. "You'll need to wait about 10 minutes before logging onto the network. You can log into the school's website with your username and password," he added.

Paul and Justin hurried to where their computers were waiting; he'd reserved them by putting his bag near them. "Glad no one took my stuff," Paul said as he sat down.

Method for Discounted Text Books

"First things first," Paul said. "Let's get you some books. I promised you that meeting with me would be financially rewarding, and now it's time to make good on my promise—starting with books. The school is pretty good about putting the class book list together online. Still, they typically wait until two days before school starts to release it publicly."

Paul directed the computer's web browser to the school website and clicked the "Sign In" link. He handed the keyboard over to Justin to type in his own username and password. Paul then went to Justin's profile and showed him how to access his book list.

"Hmm, it looks like you need to get eleven books in total," said Paul.

Justin saw a web-generated form that had a list of book titles, editions, authors, and ISBN numbers.

"How convenient," said Paul in a semi-sarcastic tone. "They list the prices in the bookstore so that you can see how much you will have to shell out. By the looks of things, your most expensive book is $122.99."

Justin couldn't believe it: the books totaled over $500. Paul must have seen the look on Justin's face as he saw the total price. "Scary, isn't it?" asked Paul in a reassuring tone. "Now, let Paul the magician do his magic and show you how to out-think the system."

"Okay," said Justin.

"Normally, I decide which classes I'm absolutely going to take in any given semester and then e-mail each teacher, weeks in advance, telling him or her that I am enrolled in their class and asking them what the book titles, authors, and ISBNs are. Then I ask, in the same email, which books are *required* and which are *optional*. I order the books from half.com or Amazon.com, along with Abebooks.com, and use Bigwords as a textbook search engine, and they get here in plenty of time. In your case, we're going to do this, but with a slight twist."

"What do you mean?" asked Justin. "School starts tomorrow; I can't pay for overnight shipping just to get a book here."

"Well," said Paul, "in your case, considering that $122.99 book on the list, overnight shipping would still be a cheaper solution than the bookstore prices."

"Are you serious?" Justin asked, surprised.

"Think about it," responded Paul. "Say we can get the book for $85 online, and it costs $30 to overnight the book to you. What is the sum of $85 + $30?" Paul asked.

"That's $115," Justin replied, realizing that the bookstore price would be $122.99, plus tax.

"Now are you beginning to see?" asked Paul. "But I think we can do *better* than an eight-dollar savings."

Paul's words really piqued Justin's interest. "Okay," he said, "now you've got me hooked. How do you do *that*?"

"Well, we happen to be in a library. Unfortunately, we're a little late. Like I mentioned, I typically have all my books shipped to me weeks in advance, but we can see what we can do. Let's look at the on-line library catalog and see if there are any books *here* that you need," Paul continued.

"And I just renew them out from the library each week! Brilliant!" Justin said excitedly as he interrupted.

"Um, no," Paul said in a polite but correcting tone. "Lots of freshmen try to do that, but the library has policies against multiple renewals of the same book. Even if they didn't, there's at least one other student who has the same idea. You end up either not being able to renew your book when you need it—say, right about midterms—or you get in a check-out war of who gets it first. In the end, it costs you time, as well as money in acquired library fines because you don't want to turn the book back in for fear that you won't have it when you need it. You can ask me how I know *that* one.

"The only exception," Paul continued, "is if the teacher reserves a copy at the library service desk; you can borrow the book for a few hours to read. Speaking from experience, that's a good option if you just need to read the book for homework."

Justin could tell that Paul knew some of the ins and outs of this college thing, especially when it came to buying books. That was one of the things that he liked about Paul, his attention to detail.

"Okay, professor, teach me," Justin said with a smile.

"We check out the books just long enough for the online shipments to get here," Paul said with a wry smile. "The post office's Media Mail option is a good one because it reduces shipping costs, and packages can typically get here before you have to return the book."

"*Nice,*" Justin said in awe, realizing he was learning from both a friend and a master of the system.

Three of Justin's books were available at the library, with one more already checked out that was due back in two weeks. Paul helped Justin place holds on all four books. "We'll grab the three books that are in today before you leave," Paul assured Justin. "Next, we need to find the books online. Let's start at half.com and Amazon.com with your booklist."

They copied the ISBN codes into the portals. To save time, they opened the books they wanted to know more about, in new tabs in an Internet browser. By this time, Justin was able to log onto his own computer, so this sped up the search.

"Here's a good one," Justin said as he was searching. "It's only about 30% of the total cost."

"Whoa!" said Paul. "'Danger, Will Robinson,'" he quoted with a grin.

"What do you mean?" Justin asked a bit confused.

"Because it's so close to the start of a semester," said Paul, "most books online go up in price. If your book is that cheap, be sure to check if it's the *international version* of the book. The international version can be a knockoff version that usually someone in a foreign country paid to have copied by some low-paid worker. The wording, pages, page numbers, graphs, and pictures often are skewed, stuff can be missing, or just wrong, and usually they're black and white, instead of colored like the original. The ink color is not so much a problem for books that are strictly text, but when it comes to pictures and graphs, you'll wish you could see what's being described. Worse than that, they're harder to sell, or resell."

Paul continued, "I know that's a mouthful, but it's important to know what you're getting before you buy it. I find it's just not honest, either: First, the company that copied the book may not have permission from the publisher, and second, the sellers dishonestly try to represent the book as the real deal. That's why you should always check the book description from the seller, and when in doubt, you can message the seller and ask. On the bright side, if the seller doesn't disclose this truth, most online companies like half.com, Amazon.com, or Abe Books will refund the money and protect the buyer."

"Good to know," Justin said.

Sure enough, the book was the international edition. Justin skipped that one. After finding all of the books online, Justin was curious why they had only opened the books in tabs on the Internet browser and had not bought any yet. Finally, his curiosity got the better of him, and he asked Paul.

"Well, we've spent a total of about 15 minutes. Add the best quality books to your shopping cart for the price in your price range, and they're reserved for about fifteen minutes so that you won't lose them to another buyer. If we stopped here, you would still be in good shape. Let's check two more spots. There's a student book exchange here at SSU. Let's look and see if any of your textbooks are there."

Justin first added the other books to his online shopping cart and then gave Paul the keyboard to direct his browser to the online book exchange. After Paul did so, Justin quickly copied and pasted the IS-BNs to the search field of the webpage. Three of his books were available, and one was about $2.50 more than the web prices that Justin had previously found, with the other two being closer to the bookstore prices.

"You should get the book that's $2.50 more," said Paul.

"Why?" asked Justin, confused as to why his friend was suggesting paying *more* for a book, when he thought he was trying to save money.

"The reason," Paul continued, "is that *this* book you can get *now*. If you add up the shipping, you're just about there, but this book you can physically *see*, and if you don't like it, you can go back to the online books. Remember, 'a bird in hand is worth two in the bush,'" Paul said.

Justin called the seller and made arrangements to see the book in about an hour. Ironically, the seller suggested that they meet in a building by the library; Paul gave directions.

"Okay," said Justin to Paul, "you mentioned there are *two* additional spots to check. Where is the second?"

"Before we go on, let's finish the first," Paul said.

Paul directed Justin to *www.bigwords.com*, and did some searches for some of the books. After finding one of the books, Paul said it was time to get the second method.

"Last, we look for digital versions of the book," he explained. "Some students are passionate about *real* books and others like the convenience of carrying most of their books with them on their Smartphone or tablet. You won't really know which you prefer until you try both. I'd recommend trying a digital book that's mostly text, and see if you like it. Most of the time digital books are cheaper than physical books, but they can't be resold, so only buy the book digitally if you can't get it cheaper as physical copy or if you wouldn't mind keeping a digital copy for yourself. Typically, I only use digital books that are under $30.00."

"How do I find a digital copy?" Justin asked.

"Go back to Half.com or Amazon.com where we found your books and open a new tab to a link that says something like 'other editions.' That's where you find them, if they exist," Paul directed.

Getting Paid for Buying Textbooks

Justin followed the instructions and found five of his books had other editions. Three of the five were old editions, one was a digital edition, and the last was a new edition that was a newer revision than what his book list from the bookstore required. The newer edition also happened to be one of the books that Justin had reserved at the library.

"Gold mine!" said Paul excitedly.

"What's a gold mine?" Justin asked.

"Look," responded Paul, "if you find a book that the campus is using repeatedly in the older edition, you can order, like, five to six extra
copies every semester and sell them for $10-15 less than the used-book
price offered at the bookstore by posting an ad on the book exchange
or by going early to class and writing your ad on the chalkboard. The
trick is to e-mail the teacher each semester and ask what books are required so that you don't get stuck with the extra books you might buy.
I did this with a book that I could get for $7 online, and I sold it for $58
to other students, since the professors continued to use the old edition.
The students were happy to get a book for $20 less than the bookstore
price, and I helped the class have ample books—*plus,* I made about
$50 per book that I sold![5] I did this for three semesters, selling about
four books a semester. I did get stuck with two unsold books one semester because I had over-ordered and hadn't marketed enough before
the campus finally updated the edition they used. But I listed and sold
the two older-edition books *at cost* on the book exchange, specifically
mentioning that the books were the former editions, so I suffered no
loss. Over three semesters, I made about $500 dollars, and I only wish
I had bought more books when I first knew about it."

"So, wait," said Justin. "You buy extra books every semester and
sell them to other students?"

"Well, yeah, why not? I help the students, and I help myself. A few
weeks in advance of the new semester, I just e-mail the professors of
the classes I'm going to take, find cheap copies of the books, get them
shipped to me, and then advertise like crazy the week before and the
week after classes start—trying to get students to buy my books by
posting on the book exchange and in classrooms directly. You'd be
surprised how many students wait until the last minute to get books."
Paul carefully didn't say 'like you.'

"I really do the same amount of work as I would have done for
myself; I just add some additional books to my order. I usually get all
of my books paid for this way, plus I earn a little extra money for each
semester," Paul said with a hint of excitement in his voice.

"That is so awesome," Justin said.

"I know," Paul responded. "Just don't tell everyone my secrets. I'm
telling *you* because you're my friend, and I think you need to learn the

5 The author really did this for multiple semesters and profited with sales.

ropes of saving money with books. Plus, I was saddened to hear about your dad and your lack of funds. You may not be able to sell any books *this* semester, but keep it in mind for later. Now that you know most of my tricks for finding cheaper books, don't make the same mistakes I made and pay inflated book prices."

"Okay," Justin responded.

After placing his orders for his online books and for a digital book that was $10, he still had to buy a campus-published workbook that was $13.99. His total was $233.47. "Wow! I saved about $260 from what I would have spent when I was at the Student Center," Justin remarked.

"I'll take a check for my commission," said Paul jokingly. "But seriously, a few hundred dollars every semester makes a big difference. I *told you* meeting with me would be worth your time."

"Thanks for your help! These past several minutes have saved me a lot of money." Justin was relieved.

"You're welcome," said Paul. "And don't worry. Soon, you'll be able to do what we did today in just about 10 minutes. I haven't told you everything, but I'm sure you can figure out some more of this on your own. Find what's honest and works and then use it to your advantage."

Paul looked at the time. "Hey, listen, I need to go meet up with my girlfriend Anna. Just be sure to get the library copies of the textbooks before you go. You'll want to get those soon so that they aren't taken by other students."

"I'll get right on it," Justin said. "Besides, I have to go meet up with the guy who I called about selling me his book."

"A few last pieces of advice," Paul said.

"What are those?" Justin asked.

Be Prepared to Make Choices—Knowing Your Options

"One, the university offers an interest-free payment plan—if you can pay for the entire balance of tuition this semester. You can pay several hundred dollars upfront, and then pay the rest over the semester if you can get a job. While it is better to pay all upfront, this helps avoid some of the costs of student loans. Check with the tuition office. Two, if you do end up absolutely needing a student loan, check with multiple places because different organizations have different rates, fees, and payment schedules. I'd recommend checking with the campus financial aid office and your bank, and then compare the two."

"Thanks for the heads up," Justin said.

"Sure thing," Paul replied.

Paul and Justin said their good-byes and parted ways. Justin entered his expenses into his Smartphone budget and then went to the librarian's desk and asked how to find the books he had placed on hold. This was by far the biggest library he had ever seen, with literally miles of rows of books on multiple floors. The librarian gave Justin a map and showed him how to find the books he needed. He spent the next 30 minutes wandering the aisles. He was grateful Paul had taken the time to show him the ropes for purchasing textbooks. After getting turned around in the library a few times, Justin was finally able to get all the books he needed.

He went to meet up with Dan, the seller from the book exchange. He still had a meeting with a counselor at 1 p.m., but at least he had most of his books, either with him or on order.

... 3148, 3150, 3154... Justin thought as he passed rooms in the building's hallway. He was looking for room 3206 where the seller had said to meet him. Justin hoped that after meeting with the school counselor, he would have time to locate the rooms where his classes were, as well as find a job and try to get a student loan. He passed rooms 3200, 3202, 3208. *Hey wait– where is 3204 and 3206?* Justin asked himself. He was at a hallway intersection and started wondering where the next numbers were. Then he saw a large glass office with the words "Campus I.T. Resources" printed across the glass. The door was open, so he decided to check with someone inside.

Types of Jobs to Get

"Hi. I'm looking for room 3206, and I was wondering if you could tell me where to go," Justin said to a cute girl, behind the reception desk, who was obviously the secretary.

"You're here," was the reply. "The I.T. office is rooms 3204 and 3206."

"I called about a book from the book exchange, and a guy named Dan told me to meet him in 3206," Justin said.

"Hold on," the secretary said. She dialed an extension on the telephone, and Justin heard a phone ring in one of the cubes in the office. The secretary spoke into the phone. "Dan, there's a guy here saying that you posted a book on the book exchange and that you told him to meet you here." Justin could faintly hear a male voice a little bit away. The secretary continued speaking with Dan on the phone. "Uh huh, okay. I'll send him over." She hung up the phone and smiled at Justin. "Just go to the fourth row over there," she said, pointing in the appropriate direction.

Justin thanked her, went around the counter in the direction she had pointed, and proceeded to the fourth row. He stopped at the cube that had "Daniel" written on a name plate. The cube was an open cube that shared space with an adjacent cube. Seated inside the cube, on opposite walls, were two guys who were just a little older than Justin.

"Are you Dan?" Justin said, hoping one of them would answer.

"I'm Jon," was the first reply.

"I'm Dan," replied the guy to Justin's left. "Are you here about the book?"

"Yeah," Justin said.

"Here it is," Dan responded, holding up a volume.

The book's cover was slightly worn, so Justin asked if he could browse through it. Dan agreed that he could.

As Justin was looking at the book, an older gentleman hurriedly came in and addressed Jon. "Jon, did you hear that Stewart said he couldn't work this semester because he was accepted as a biology TA? We need to find someone to take his place and work his shift," the man continued.

"Do you want me to call Student Services and post the job?" asked Jon.

At the mention of the word "job," Justin's attention turned to the conversation he was hearing. "Do you think we can get someone to cover for him until we get a replacement?" Justin heard Jon say to the older gentleman.

"Excuse me," said Justin, turning to face them. "I couldn't help overhearing. Did you say that you need to find someone to cover a shift? I'm looking for a job. What position are you talking about?"

The older man turned to him. "We are talking about the computer lab monitor."

"A what...?" Justin asked.

"Have you seen the computer help desks or information desks at the library?" asked the man.

"Yes. A guy there helped me earlier this morning," replied Justin.

"Well, there are computer labs all over campus," said the man, "and we need to have someone in each lab to help people with their computers, word processing, and Internet access. The people in the labs are called computer lab monitors. If there is no lab monitor, campus policy requires us to close the computer lab. We need to find someone to cover the computer lab at the MK Building between 2:30 and 6:00 in the afternoon, Monday through Friday... What experience do you have with computers?"

Justin wasn't sure where the MK Building was, but he certainly knew how to surf the Internet and use MS Word and Excel, and the hours would work out well with his classes.

"I worked as a tour guide in Alaska," answered Justin, "and used the computer system on the tours and to file reports. I also worked in an office as part of a humanitarian project in Ecuador."

"Okay," said the older gentleman. He asked Justin a few basic questions about his experience and then said, "If you can agree to start today, and if you pass our basic computer literacy test, you can have the position. It's minimum campus wage, which is about a dollar per hour higher than the national minimum wage."

"Where do I take the literacy test?" Justin inquired.

"Jon can get you started and take down your information," the man responded. "By the way, I'm Kevin Markus."

"I'm Justin Murray."

Mr. Markus turned to Jon and said, "Get Justin started on the basic computer literacy test, and then if he doesn't pass, post a job at Student Services so that we can get this filled—but it has got to be done ASAP. I need to go finish a project for the CS department."

"Will do," said Jon.

Mr. Markus then excused himself, and Dan piped up in a joking tone: "So, you gonna buy the book?"

Justin laughed. "Yeah, I guess I will." He wrote out a check and put the book in his backpack.

Jon showed where Justin could use a computer to take the test. The test took about 30 minutes, and Justin passed. Some of the questions were: "How do you open a new tab in an Internet browser?" and "How do you set text in a 'bold' font?"

Jon took Justin's personal information for the job and told him that he had been lucky to be in the right place at the right time. Jon then gave Justin the room number for the computer lab in the MK Building where he needed to go.

"Just be there before 2 p.m. and I can show you the ropes on helping people," Jon said.

"Do I need to walk up and down the aisles and find who needs help?" Justin asked, trying to clarify his duties.

"No," Jon replied, "just sit at the desk and wait for someone to ask for your help."

"What do I do when no one comes to ask for help?" Justin asked.

"Some of our lab monitors read, others surf the web, others do homework or whatever—as long as you obey lab rules," Jon remarked.

Justin remembered the information-desk attendant in the library earlier that day who had been reading when Justin walked by. He then realized just how good a job he had gotten: he would be getting paid to do his homework.

By then it was 10:30. Justin went to the building where a financial counselor could meet with him. There was a long line, of other students. The setting kind of reminded Justin of the DMV, where people would be "cattle called" when an available attendant was ready. There was a sign above a computer that read: "Hate to wait? Sign up for an appointment."

Justin didn't have time to wait because he had an appointment with the school counselor. After waiting for several students to use the computer, Justin made an appointment; the only time that was available was for Friday at 11 a.m. Justin decided to schedule a time to meet with a counselor instead of waiting—in the meantime, he hoped to meet with his bank to explore options.

Justin had a quick PB&J sandwich from his backpack and headed to his appointment with the counselor. Justin was assigned a counselor by the name of Ms. Crawford. When he was invited to her desk, she asked, "What can I do for you?"

"I just need to make sure that I have enough classes to be enrolled full time," Justin said.

Ms. Crawford asked for his information and pulled up his profile. "It looks like you need to have two more credits to be a full time student. What classes do you want to take?"

"Do you have any classes like racquetball or tennis?" Justin asked, remembering Dave's advice to get fun classes.

"Hmm, the P.E. classes are only one credit, so you will need to take two of them," Ms. Crawford said.

"Okay. So, are any available?" Justin asked hopefully.

"There are two openings, one at 3 p.m. and one at 5 p.m.," Ms. Crawford replied.

Justin recalled his job from 2:30 to 6:30 and realized this wouldn't work. "I have to work then. What else do you have?"

"Ballet and floor gymnastics are available."

Justin frowned, Ms. Crawford continued speaking.

"Most of the entry-level classes are full and based on your student standing and work schedule you don't have many options. But there are two 7 a.m. classes that could work. One is woodcarving, and the other is a class that opened up just today, a personal finance class."

The counselor told Justin that the woodcarving class would deal with using blocks of wood for lathing and for making figurines. The finance class was a specialty class that was going to be taught by a visiting professor.

Woodcarving sounded like a lot of fun, Justin thought. He had always wanted to learn how to make things with wood. He imagined himself carving birds and fish for his family and maybe for a girlfriend later. He decided to take it.

"I'll take the..." Justin began, but just then the words his grandfather had spoken to him came to mind:

You're at an important time in your life, Justin; learn all that you can about money and how it works. You're at a time of choice and decision. The habits that you establish now will go with you for a good portion of your life.

"Yes?" said Ms. Crawford, trying to evoke a response.

"I'll take the personal finance class," Justin said hesitantly and with a hint of longing in his voice for missing out on the "fun" class.

Chapter 2: Principles and Suggestions

1. Buying Books:

   a. Go to *www.CollegeCashChampion.com* to see videos on how to do this.

   b. Contact the professors for each of the classes that you plan to take, three or four weeks prior to the start of the semester. Ask for the ISBN.

   c. Go to two or three online websites that sell books. I recommend: half.com, Amazon.com, and Abebooks.com, with Bigwords.com as a search engine, although there are others. Type the ISBN into the search engine.

      i. Check the description. Avoid international editions.

      ii. Check the time frame for shipping. Know your deadlines.

iii. Check the base price + taxes + shipping. Does it fit your budget?

iv. If you need a textbook while you wait for yours to arrive, check if the book is in your school's library or the local public library. You can usually check online.

   • If you do borrow the textbook from a library, the author recommends not trying to renew the book all semester long, as there could be a library policy against this or another student who competes with you.

   • If the teacher has reserved a copy of the textbook at the library for students to use, this could work to read for a few hours.

v. If the total book price online, including tax and shipping (weeks before the start of a semester), is a good deal and is lower than the bookstore's respective new/used prices by at least $15 for used and $20 for new, then consider buying three to five copies of the book and reselling them.

vi. If your campus uses an older edition of a book that has a newer edition, this is a good time to cash in on the difference. **However**, this does require that you have verified the exact books and editions with the professor(s) of the classes for which you are anticipating buying extra books that semester. Otherwise, you might purchase too many old editions.

   • Compared to buying in the bookstores, buying older editions of textbooks online is much cheaper. Usually, you will save about $50 per book on science and math textbooks and $30 per book on reading books.

   • If you do accidentally buy too many books online, cut your selling price down above your total cost (book price + shipping + taxes). Often other students don't mind the older editions and will buy them from you for a really good deal; this way, you cut down on extra books and don't incur any losses.

2. Jobs that Pay Big—don't overlook a job to pay for school:

There are lots of jobs that don't require you to do much besides just be there. These jobs are valuable because, if you are allowed to do other things while at work, you can do your homework there. The way I look at it, you will need to spend the time doing homework anyway; you might as well get *paid* to do it. Think of it as a scholarship to do homework.

Here is a list of potential jobs to look at that *might* allow you to do your homework in down time (please check with each position individually):

- Teaching Assistant—when students don't come for help, there is time.
- Lab Attendant—when no one needs your help.
- Computer Lab Monitor—people will often do their own thing and will not need your help.
- Information Desk Attendants—each is different, but check.
- Receptionist at a hotel/motel—just being there is often all that is required when not checking people in.
- Night shift positions—often, night shifts are less busy; not recommended if you have early-morning class schedules.

Listening to Audios

If your class requires you to listen to lectures or if it has audio recordings (e.g., music classes), in addition to the above jobs, consider these:

- Janitors—you can listen to your MP3 player.
- Facilities—less likely, but sometimes you can get time.

Get more positions as a handout by going to: *www.CollegeCashChampion.com*

3. Personal Finance:

a. Take classes that teach you about personal finance early in your college program. These classes will help you understand how money works and how to prevent a lot of student debt.

   i.   Look at classes that will help with budgeting and wealth-creation classes.

Chapter 2: Warnings and Avoidance

1. Avoid paying too much for books. Research, ask the professor, buy online, rent, etc.

2. Don't assume that you can do homework at work. You need to check with your employer.

Chapter 3: Professor Christensen

Ms. Crawford, the counselor, explained that there was a special stipulation with the personal finance class. The instructor, a visiting professor, required each student to get his final approval before they could join the class. Justin was determined to get that signature. The class fit Justin's schedule and, ironically enough, fulfilled a beginning level math credit; he was going to take it. But first, work: Justin went to the MK Building, and there he met Jon, who showed him where to sit and how to log into the time-keeping system. He pointed out a poster that had the lab rules listed for all to see.

"Your job is to offer help to students who ask," said Jon. "About once every 1-2 hours, push the chairs in under the computer tables to help keep the lab orderly."

Justin was also given the lab code and told that there were several codes that opened the labs.

"Don't give the code to anyone," Jon told Justin "This code is tied directly to you, so if it ever gets out, you're responsible financially for anything missing or damaged.

Jon stayed in the lab to show Justin some more of the ropes, but after 30 minutes, he had to get back to the Student I.T. room to handle things there.

The MK Building was not in the central part of campus, but still had many students who needed to use the lab. A few students asked Justin for help with getting on the Internet. He wondered how they had missed acquiring such a simple skill.

Justin wasn't allowed to talk on his cell phone during work, so he logged in to his e-mail. He checked his e-mail and then tried to study a map of the campus so he could find his classes later. By the third long, boring hour of his shift, he remembered the attendant who had been reading at the information desk in the library and wished he had brought an interesting book—good thing he would have homework to occupy him in the future.

Justin logged into his bank account and started a chat session to see if he could speak with a representative about getting a student loan. The representative told him that he would have to make an appointment and come in person or speak over the phone. All of the appointments were full for the next two days. Justin thanked the rep and ended the chat.

School was starting tomorrow, with his first class at 7 a.m. *Why did I take a 7 a.m. class and why one that has math? Maybe I should have gone with woodworking. How am I going to pay for school? Why is this so difficult?*

The rest of the afternoon was uneventful. At the end of his shift, Justin met his replacement for the next shift, a girl named Erin. Justin and she spoke for a little bit.

"Yeah, I've had this job for three semesters," Erin said. "It's kind of nice to get paid to do my homework, and believe me: my major has a lot of homework."

Paul had previously invited Justin to a movie at his place, and Justin wanted to go see it—especially since he had missed the dance. He went back to his car and found a pink "Parking Violation" notice under his windshield wiper. He realized that he had inadvertently parked in a row reserved for administrative parking, which was just opposite of the row for visitor parking. *I bet they hide the signs on purpose,* Justin thought, more than a little annoyed. The violation ticket stated, as a reminder, that parking passes could be purchased at the Campus Traffic and Parking Center.

When he got to the apartment, he saw Paul with a girl that he guessed was Anna, along with several other people.

"Dude!" said Paul. "Glad you could come."

"So am I," said Justin.

"Grab some snacks," Paul said, pointing to a table containing some chips, salsa, cakes, and other goodies.

Justin's alarm rang at 6:15 a.m. *Ugh, why did I stay up past 11:30? Maybe a 7 a.m. class isn't such a good idea.* Justin got dressed, read, and went downstairs.

"Heard you come in last night," Dave said to Justin. "Would you mind coming in closer to 10:15 so that you don't wake us up when you get in?"

"Sorry," Justin said a little sheepishly. "I'll do better."

"So, did you get any *fun* classes?" Dave asked in a curious tone.

"They were mostly all taken," Justin said.

"Mostly?" Dave asked skeptically. "What do you mean *mostly*?"

"Well, I had the choice between this financial math class and wood-working," Justin clarified.

"You traded woodworking for a math class?" Dave said with surprise. "I'm telling you, man, the fun classes are the ones that you need to be takin'. You'll thank me later."

"'Kay, thanks," Justin said. "I've got to go."

Justin had hoped that he could quickly ask the professor to sign his Add/Drop card if he arrived early. He found the class and sat in the second row. There were 15 other students at the desks. The teacher was at his desk, not looking at anyone, finishing something on the computer. The hourly bell rang, and the professor rose from his desk.

Very sternly the professor said "Class, I am Professor Christensen, *and* I will be addressed as such."

The professor clicked a button on the remote in his hand, and the overhead projector turned on. A PowerPoint was visible and had the words "Today's Agenda" written across the slide. The screen changed and there was a bulleted list that included the following:

- Class rules

- Syllabus

- Grading

"Rule number one," Professor Christensen announced as the slide changed. "*Nothing* late will be accepted."

As he was speaking, two more students filed in. "Ah, just in time," said Professor Christensen snidely. "We are discussing class rules, and we are on the topic of being late."

"'Kay, whatever," said one of the students who was late.

"We haven't gotten there yet, but you all will still need a signature from me to add this class and without it, you will *not* be taking this class. The world is full of people who think that they are entitled to privileges above others. Let me be clear, this class is not going to be an easy class. You won't be able to just sit in, show up, and get an 'A.' As it is with life, so it will be with this class: any privileges you enjoy are ones that either are given to you by others or are earned. However, this will be a rewarding class."

"Some of you will come here and just try to squeak by," Professor Christensen continued. "That is not the way that I am going to be running this class. That is why rule number one is: Nothing late will be accepted. Some of you will work for an employer, and hopefully you will *not* one day say to your boss, 'Gee, boss, I know that I didn't get the analysis report in on time and that as a result, we lost the prestigious Johnson account we were going to get, but here's the report, though late, done the way you asked, at least I hope it is done the way you wanted. You can now go to Mr. Johnson and ask him if we can have partial credit for trying to get things done the way we promised we would.'"

"If anyone ever has that conversation with his or her boss, I hope that your résumé is polished and ready to go, because your job is very much in jeopardy. Life doesn't usually allow make-ups or partial credit. Sometimes it will, but most of the time, it will not. *If you are not ready to catch opportunity when it comes, then opportunity will not catch you,*" Professor Christensen said with emphasis.

"Don't you mean that no late *work* will be accepted, instead of nothing late will be accepted?" asked a male student from behind Justin.

"No, I mean that with class, *nothing* late will be accepted. This includes anyone who comes late to class. You see, most days we will be going on a field trip, and we will leave right at 7 a.m. If you are not here, then you are not coming. Additionally, I will be locking the door at 7. If you are not in the room, you will miss the discussion and the assignments. And for anyone who thinks he or she can just ask your classmates which assignments are the ones needed for any particular day, believe me: I will check your attendance. All assignments are due either at the beginning of class or on the deadline specified on the class website."

Professor Christensen then clicked the remote in his hand to advance the slide. The following rules came on the PowerPoint:

- Rule #1: <u>Nothing</u> late will be accepted. No exception.
- Rule #2: We respect each other and each other's beliefs.
- Rule #3: All submitted work is final. No "redo" chances!
- Rule #4: Class participation is mandatory for the grade.
- Rule #5: We act with integrity in everything we do; we do not allow anyone to do anything that would violate personal integrity or class rules.
- Rule #6: If we need help, we ask for help.
- Rule #7: If someone asks us for help, we help.
- Rule #8: We maintain positive attitudes.
- Rule #9: We take good care of our bodies, minds, and spirits.
- Rule #10: We express gratitude for all help we receive.

"Any questions?" Professor Christensen asked the class.

"What if we have a school-excused absence or are sick when class meets? Shouldn't we be allowed to make up work?" asked a girl to the right of Justin.

"If you're going to be absent on a class day," answered the professor, "you will need to finish and submit the assignments before you go. Most athletes know when games, practices, and out-of-school events are held. You will need to notify me before the fact. As for being sick, you had better get a doctor's note and be bedridden. Remember rule number nine: We take good care of our bodies, minds, and spirits."

"What constitutes acting with integrity? How are you going to know whether or not we didn't act with integrity?" asked a guy on the far right of the classroom.

The professor's gaze settled on him firmly when he responded: "There are certain principles and laws in this universe. Sir Isaac Newton said, 'For every action, there is an equal and opposite reaction.' This principle applies to things physical and in every-day life. In reference to people, you cannot acquire true wealth by being dishonest. I will know by how you respond and how the universe responds to you. This means that if you try to cheat in other classes, lie to someone else, or act with dishonesty, you'll soon find that others will not trust you, your relationships will suffer, and you will lower your own self-esteem and self-value.

"*You must act with honor to receive honorable gains*; anything else destroys happiness and lessens your wealth, cheapens your own self-respect, and burdens you with guilt. True, many people cheat and lie to get money fraudulently, but those people do not have true wealth, and they lessen their experiences in life and their interpersonal relationships, and future opportunities.

"Mark Victor Hansen and Robert G. Allen invite us to become one of the Enlightened Millionaire Club.[6] To get there, we can only do those things which leave everyone better off than how we found them and enhance humanity in the process. I will be teaching you the principles of how to acquire wealth. While you may get money by being dishonest, *true wealth comes by increasing quality of life in every area of your life*—and your character is part of your wealth. As Isaac Newton said: 'For every action, there is an equal and opposite reaction.'"[7]

"If we treat others harshly, others will oppose us harshly. When we are honest in all areas of our lives and act with integrity, we are entitled to help from God and the universe. I know that many of you may not believe in God; I'm not asking you to change your beliefs, but don't try to silence my beliefs. Each of us has the right to express our beliefs and that shouldn't offend anyone. If someone tells you: 'Good Luck!'

6 Hansen, Mark Victor and Robert G. Allen. *The One Minute Millionaire: The Enlightened Way to Wealth.* New York: Three Rivers Press, 2009.

7 The Physics Classroom. "Newton's Third Law." Accessed April 19, 2014. http://www.physicsclassroom.com/class/newtlaws/Lesson-4/Newton-s-Third-Law.

Even if you don't believe in luck, it shouldn't offend you that someone wishes you well. Consider any reference I make to God in the same way. We can still learn from others' beliefs that may differ from our own, even if we may not agree on every point. I don't believe Aesop's fables literally, but I still value the lessons they teach me, and I am not offended when I hear '*The Tortoise and the Hare*' even if I doubt that such a race ever occurred. In this class, we'll respect the beliefs of every individual in the class. I will use anything from poetry to ancient texts, if I feel that it will help teach a financial concept."

Professor Christensen continued his lecture. "Next is the syllabus portion of the class," He clicked the button in his hand:

- Real Estate
- Business
- Scholarships and Grants
- Money Smarts
- Banking
- Online Models
- Investing
- Money Seeds

"Don't worry too much about these points right now; we'll cover all of them," said Professor Christensen. "Let me show you how grading works." He advanced the slide again:

- Assignments: 35%
- Class Participation: 10%
- Teacher Evaluation: 55%—Ongoing and completely subjective questions and evaluations given throughout the semester and at the end of the term.

"What!" cried several students.

"What do you mean, it's subjective and ongoing?" one of the class members dared to ask.

"It means," responded Professor Christensen, "that as per your question earlier about integrity, if I learn that you were dishonest in an area of your life: that you cheated, lied, acted disrespectful towards another's beliefs, broke another rule, and/or chose to intentionally neglect an assignment, I have the right to sink 55% of your grade as low as I desire. I get to decide how you fare, based completely subjective to my evaluation. You can try to 'scrape by' but all it will take is one dishonest event and your grade is over. This is my class, and here the rules are made in response to how life works and what the universe teaches about abundance. If anyone here doesn't want to abide by these rules and this grading system, there is the door," Professor Christensen pointed at the classroom door.

With those words, the same student packed up his stuff and huffed out the door, mumbling something about "I'm not leaving my grade up to chance from a whimsical tyrant who won't even give me a fair grading scale…"

Professor Christensen smiled. "I love it when they do that," he said wryly. "Anyone else? You might as well leave now because this course is not going to get any easier," he continued with an expectant look on his face.

Two more students got up and left. Professor Christensen's smile widened with the kind of smile that made you wonder if he enjoyed watching students suffer. Justin thought about his woodworking class again. *Maybe this is a bad idea, to take this class*. As he was contemplating, his thoughts were interrupted by Professor Christensen.

The professor asked the class, "Do you think those students were victors or victims? Do you think they were people who chose to *act*, or to be acted *upon*[8] by life and circumstances? Do you think they blamed me and the class, or were willing to take responsibility for their own thoughts, emotions, and actions?"

"Victims," came a reply from a girl in the back of the class. Justin turned to look at the girl speaking and saw that she was *really* cute.

"Attitude is a choice, and they chose to point to others for their emotions," the girl added.

"Very good," said Professor Christensen. "Victor Frankl said: 'The one thing you can't take away from me is the way I choose to respond to what you do to me. The last of one's freedoms is to choose one's

---

8 See 2 Nephi 2:14

attitude in any given circumstance.'[9] Sadly, most people choose to give this freedom away first; they let other people and circumstances control how they respond, rather than choosing for themselves. As Ms.—" Professor Christensen paused, trying to evoke a name, gesturing towards the girl who had spoken.

"Pratt, Allison Pratt," the girl responded.

"As Ms. Pratt said, 'Attitude is a choice,'" Professor Christensen said. Instantly the mood in the room changed, going from a feeling of self-pity to wonder. "We will come back to this point later, but this brings us to rule number 11," Professor Christensen said as he changed the slide on the PowerPoint. "We take full responsibility for our thoughts, emotions, actions, and results," he read aloud.

Introduction to Real Estate

"Now, enough jibber-jabber," Professor Christensen said. "Let's get on to today's lesson." He changed the slide: *Real Estate*. "Who here owns his or her own home?" Professor Christensen asked, raising his own hand.

Not a single hand went up. Justin looked around the room and imagined crickets chirping. "'Buehler, Buehler…'" Professor Christensen quoted coldly. "Okay, tell me why *not*."

"Uh… we're students and we have no money," a girl offered hesitantly.

Professor Christensen wrote on the chalkboard:

•   Students

•   Have no money

"Why else?" he asked. "Think deeper."

"We have no income to buy a house, and we'd lose the house," came a reply from a guy towards the front.

"Why else?" Professor Christensen asked. "That's really the same thing as having no money."

"We don't know how," another male student said.

9 Google Books. "Man's Search for Meaning - Viktor Emil Frankl." Accessed April 19, 2014. http://books.google.com/books?id=F-Q_xGjWBi8C.

"Good," said Professor Christensen, turning and expanding the list on the board:

- Students
- Have no money
- Have no income
- Don't know how

Justin decided to speak up and said, "Either the seller won't take us seriously, or the bank won't make a loan because we're college students."

Another girl also spoke up. "We may not know how to do repairs."

"Good," repeated Professor Christensen, still cold. He expanded the list on the chalkboard to read:

- Students
- Have no money
- Have no income
- Don't know how
- Seller won't believe you
- Bank won't lend to college students
- Don't know how to do repairs

"Any other reasons?" Professor Christensen asked.

Someone spoke up with a hint of sarcasm. "We'd burn the place down." Justin saw that the spikey-haired guy had answered.

"That could be a possibility," Professor Christensen said. "Why else?"

"Most places in the area are being rented."

"We might get ripped off by a seller who wants to take advantage of our being college students."

"We might lose money because we don't know what we're doing, and because we made a mistake, ruin our futures."

"We'd be stuck living here in Syracuse."

"We are already under a rent contract."

Professor Christensen added these responses to the list. He then wrote the word "Excuses" at the top so that the board looked like this:

Excuses

- Students
- Have no money
- Have no income
- Don't know how
- Seller won't believe you
- Bank won't lend to college students
- Get ripped off
- Lose money
- Ruin Future
- Don't know how to do repairs
- Burn the place down
- Most places are being rented
- Stuck living in a college town
- Locked into present renting contract

"We're going to talk about these excuses and see if we can't offer alternatives that may change your mind," Professor Christensen said. "All of the unmarried, single students answer the following questions: How much are you paying per month on rent, and is it shared or private rooms?"

Justin listened as other students spoke because he still needed to find a place to live. "$255 shared room." "$285, shared." "$390, private." "$410, private room." "$235, shared."

"Okay," said the professor. "Now, could we say that the approximate average for a shared bedroom is $250, and for a private room $350-$400? Obviously, if you choose to go to a different school, those numbers will change, but keep with the example. Those numbers were the averages that I had estimated earlier. Let's say that you wanted to buy an average, three-bedroom, two-bath house, a moderate distance from the university. Now watch the slides."

"For having two to four roommates, you can, in theory, have a house for about $142,000. I say 'in theory' because a lender wants to see a better ratio than one-to-one,

Getting a House

Shared @ $250/month	Private @ $400/month
Bedroom #1 = You	Bedroom #1 = You
Bedroom #2 = 2 roommates @ $250/month each	Bedroom #2 = 1 roommate @ $400/month
Bedroom #3 = 2 roommates @ $250/month each	Bedroom #2 = 1 roommate @ $400/month
Total $1,000 each month	Total $800 each month

With $700 each month and 4% interest, you can in theory afford a house approximately costing $142,00

(Assuming 3% closing costs and additional servicing fees.)

where you pay all of your income into a loan. I know that I didn't use all of the money, but I'll explain why in a later class. For now, suffice it to say that you can own a house and not pay rent yourself." Professor Christensen said with a smile.

Justin realized the point being made: *You don't have to be the one to have the money to make the mortgage payments.*

"Now," said the professor, "what if we were to get a house that had six bedrooms and two or three baths?" He advanced the slides on the PowerPoint again.

"In this example," said Professor Christensen, "for five to ten roommates, you could buy a really expensive house. I'm not advocating that you go and get a really expensive house—just one that you could purchase and then have the tenants, your roommates, pay the mortgage for you. The less expensive the house, and the more *quality* tenants you get, the more money you will make.

"I want you to be careful not to take this too far. Even in the example presented here, I don't really know of anyone that would like to have 10 roommates. Furthermore, I don't know that having 10 roommates is allowed by the city, as they have an ordinance on how many non-related people can live together in the same residence. In a future class, I will show you how you can apply the *concept* of having 10 roommates, without actually *having* 10 roommates—having the ten-

ants pay the mortgage."
(For more information
on this concept, see *Winning the Money Game in
College: Real Estate.*)

A girl raised her
hand and asked, "Isn't
this a little far-fetched?
I mean, you're assuming
that we had the money
in the first place to buy
the house, to make the
down payment. Most of
us are working for close
to minimum wage, and

Getting a House

Shared @ $250/month	Private @ $400/month
Bedroom #1 = You	Bedroom #1 = You
Bedroom #2-6= 10 roommates @ $250/month each	Bedroom #2-6 = 5 roommates @ $400/month each
Total $2,500 each month	Total $2,000 each month

With $1,700 each month and 4% interest, you can in
theory afford a house approximately costing $365,500

(Assuming 3% closing costs and additional servicing fees.)

we're not able to save that much money in our time at college."

"Does being a student stop you from buying a house?" Professor
Christensen asked.

"Well, no—I mean, yes. There is no way that I could afford a house
right now," responded the girl.

"As long as you believe that, you will not be able to do so because
you will stop yourself," Professor Christensen gently chided her. "Remember rule number 8, about keeping a positive attitude.

"If you want to stay in this class, you will need my signature on an
Add/Drop card," Professor Christensen went on in a tone of authority."

The spikey-haired guy raised his hand and said arrogantly, "Look,
I'm already under contract for renting a very expensive apartment.
There is no way that I'm going to waste my time looking for another
place to live when I can't even change where I live, even if I wanted
to." Several other students nodded in agreement.

"That's fine," said Professor Christensen. "I really couldn't care
less if you actually change your place of residence. However, like any
other class, this class comes with assignments, and if you want to be in
this one, you need to do this before Saturday at 8 p.m. If you haven't
done these assignments by Saturday, and the ones that I'm going to
give you in a moment, don't bother showing up Monday morning. I'm

not teaching a class on how to make excuses. I'm teaching a class on building wealth. Go cry to your girlfriend, sing a sob story to your parents, and report me to the Department Head and Dean of the University. Not a one of them will get me to change my mind on this topic, and not a one of them can ensure you a seat in my class."

"Do you have any idea who I am?" asked the guy who was being challenged.

"Yes," said Professor Christensen, "you are a temporary student in my class."

"My father is Dan Fredrickson, head partner at Fredrickson, Beecher, and Grant, LLP, city councilman, and sits on the university board," the guy said arrogantly.

"That's not who you are," said the Professor. "A moment ago you asked me if I knew who *you* were, not your father. Everything you just told me is about you riding on your father's good name and your father's hard work. Do you expect to coast through life riding on the coattails, good name, and fortune of your father? If that's your hope, you need to leave my class."

"I can't leave!" shouted the spikey-haired guy. "My father, for some strange reason, said that I had to take this class—but I don't have to like it."

"Oh, *poor baby*," said the professor sarcastically.

There was an obvious tension in the room, and Justin was feeling uncomfortable. He took a breath, raised his hand, and said, "Excuse me, Professor. With no disrespect, aren't you breaking your own rules about keeping a positive attitude and possibly the one about another's beliefs by going off on him?"

Something happened that made Justin wonder. Professor Christensen had a twinge of a smile, as though he were trying to stifle laughter. Justin couldn't tell if the professor was relishing the moment or trying *not* to enjoy the students in the class suffering. The professor looked coldly at Justin.

"What is your name?" the professor asked Justin, trying to maintain composure.

"Justin Murray." He spoke up with as much confidence as he could muster.

"You are on dangerous ground, Mr. Murray," Professor Christensen said. "Nevertheless, we need to move on to the assignments." The professor advanced the slides on the PowerPoint. The tension was gone, just like that.

Assignment Set 1:

1. Go to www.fafsa.gov/

    a. Fill out a profile with the Free Application for Federal Student Aid or FAFSA.

    b. Do a screen capture of the completed submission number—you may mask any personal information.

    c. Submit the profile on the class website.

The above listed requirement must be done before the next requirements; for the next requirements to work, many of the websites require a FAFSA application to be filled out prior to attempting a submission.

Assignment Set 2:

For the following two assignments, the Campus Student Writing Center may be helpful for any reports, essays, or submissions. Get a writing TA to review your work.

Choose one or both of the following:

1. Go to *https://bigfuture.collegeboard.org/scholarship-search* or *www.fastweb.com*; fill out a profile.

    a. Search for scholarships.

    b. Click the respective links for scholarships to two different scholarships.

    c. Read the scholarship requirements.

    d. Choose **TWO** scholarships, go to the respective scholarship websites.

    e. Apply to **TWO** different scholarships

     i.   Save a copy of what you submitted (i.e. essays, photos, etc.) and the scholarship requirements in separate files in a folder on your computer, portable hard drive, or web drive.

     ii.   It may be beneficial to make a folder on your computer for Scholarships and, if you desire, within this folder, make sub-folders for different scholarships.

     iii.   Recommended: In the folder name include the month and year, the provider of the scholarship, and the word "scholarship." Having all this information included will help you find this information later.

2. Go to the Campus Scholarship Department and/or the department for your major.

   a. Schedule an appointment with a counselor.

   b. Ask about scholarships that may be available for you based on your student profile.

   c. Get the requirements for any scholarships that you potentially qualify for.

     i.   Follow the instructions given to you by your counselor.

     ii.   More than likely, you will go to a website to submit.

     iii.   Either provide a confirmation of the submission, or

     iv.   Copy the scholarship requirements and work you are submitting (i.e. essay or photo) if by mail.

   d. Fill out a profile as listed above in #1, at https://bigfuture.collegeboard.org/scholarship-search or going to www.fastweb.com.

   e. Submit **ONE** scholarship following the previously mentioned steps in #1 and submit a screen shot.

Professor Christensen announced to the class, "Please take note that you will only be able to make submissions up to Saturday night at 8 p.m. After that, if you have not finished and submitted all assignments, you will not be in the class."

He changed the PowerPoint slide. It read:

Assignment Set 3:

1. Pick a charity to give 10% of your income.

2. Decide upon 1-5 activities that you can do to give 5 hours of service every week. Things that count as service are as follows, ALL MUST BE UNPAID:

- Unpaid religious service
- Yard care/ Snow Removal
- Helping with a campus event
- Other activity approved by instructor
- Tutoring someone
- Babysitting
- Picking up debris
- Visiting an elderly-care facility or hospital
- Volunteering at the Campus Service Center

Make a plan on how you will complete the two previous assignments. You do NOT need to do them this week UNLESS you CHOOSE. Submit your plan on the class website by Saturday at 8 p.m.

"There is no class on Friday this week," Professor Christensen announced. "Remember to do these four assignment sets. Those who do these assignments by Saturday at 8 p.m. and who arrive Monday before 7 a.m. will be added to the class on Monday."

"Wait—isn't Monday the Add/Drop deadline for classes?" a girl behind Justin asked.

"My, you are perceptive," said Professor Christensen. "You're going to have to take a chance," he continued in a cold tone. "If you want to be in this class, you need to decide now. I am not going to make it easy for you. It's going to be a grueling semester, and you may wonder why you ever decided to take me as a professor. Yet, if you do what I've outlined, it will be very rewarding. You know the class rules. You have seen how I interact with others. You should know that I have NO tolerance for dinking around nor for work that is less than your best."

There was an audible silence in the room. The hourly bell rang; it was now 8:50 a.m.—the end of a two-hour block.

Justin and the other students got up from their desks and packed their belongings slowly. As Justin was packing his things, the Professor said, "Just a minute, Mr. Murray. I need to speak with you before you go."

A guy passing Justin overheard and said, "If he tries to get you to do a *Heil Hitler*, remind him this is America and we have something here called courtesy."

Justin answered under his breath with a hint of sarcasm, "Thanks."

Chapter 3: Principles and Suggestions

1. Keep the rules that are listed from the class in your daily life.

2. Start to think in new ways. Just because you're a student doesn't mean you need to do things the same ways everyone else does.

3. Be willing to stand up for your beliefs. No one has the right to criticize your self-worth and integrity. Often, by speaking up, you put an end to the bullying.

Chapter 3: Warnings and Avoidance

1. Don't go buy real estate yet. Read: Winning the Money Game in College: Real Estate, you will learn some principles that will greatly help you."

2. To apply for scholarships, do your best to keep your GPA up. It will help you greatly in receiving these gifts offered to students.

3. Remember always to get legal and professional advice before making any financial decision. You can find some great ways to get discounted legal advice at *www.CollegeCashChampion.com*.

Chapter 4: The Proof is in the Pudding

Justin didn't know why Professor Christensen wanted to speak with him. Still, he dutifully made his way to the front of the classroom and stopped in front of the professor, who looked him right in the eye.

"Mr. Murray," Professor Christensen said, as cold as ever, "that was a very brave thing that you did earlier—standing up for someone whom you may not even know."

"Well, I—" Justin started, but he was cut off.

"I don't want to hear any excuses. However, I am going to give you some information that may be of use to you. First, I would like you to take this class. I admire people who can stand up for others and hold fast to their principles. Second, things are not always what they seem; in order to find gold, you often have to search for it in places where other people are afraid to venture or may not think to look. You may go now, Mr. Murray," the professor dismissed bluntly as he gestured towards the door.

Justin walked away confused. *What was that all about?* Justin asked himself as he made his way to his next class. *Why did the professor ask to see me? What did he mean when he said that he wanted me to take this class when he seems so rude and abrupt and like a jerk? Does he want to pick a fight with me all semester? I mean, what's this guy's problem? We're just students, and he was picking a fight with nearly anyone who offered any opinion. I still need to pay for school. Why am I taking this class anyway?*

Justin's next class passed with much less drama and presentation from the teacher. In fact, it was kind of boring; most of the class time was spent going over the syllabus and grading policies. Justin realized that, come Monday, he was going to have to *run* from Professor Christensen's class in order to submit his Add/Drop card and get to his next class on time. *Well,* he thought, *if the class turns out to be a disaster, at least there's that cute girl...*

Justin's third class passed about the same way as the other—no drama and a lot of logistical information. He had a thirty-minute break before his next class; he figured that he would call his bank to see about getting a student loan.

Some Downsides to Student Loans

"Let me be clear about some things," the representative from Justin's bank said, "You will not be able to rid yourself of the loan. Even if you were to declare bankruptcy; you would still be responsible for the loan amount. Interest will still accrue during the time that you are in school. At any point that you stop going to school, you will start the payment clock where you will be required to start making payments to pay back the loan with interest accumulated. Having a student loan may hinder you from getting additional loans, including but not limited to, a mortgage or auto loan. This is a serious financial obligation that may permanently affect you. Do you wish to continue with the loan?"

Justin gave his information stating that he would be attending at least full time. The representative gave him the loan rate, payback schedule if he finished his schooling as planned. "Would you like to borrow money to pay for things like rent and living costs?"

Wait! Justin thought, *Paul said to at least compare options. Before I sign my life away, I should at least keep my appointment with the school financial counselor.* "I am meeting with a financial counselor from the school on Friday. Now that I know what you are offering, may I come into a local branch if your offer is better?"

"That will be fine," the rep said. They ended the call.

At least I can check to see who offers me a better deal. Justin thought as he hung up the phone. *Can never be dismissed? Interest accrues while in school—so the balance keeps going up?! May hinder my financial future?! What kind of service is that? That seems more like slavery. I had better be careful before I sign up for a student loan. I'm glad Paul at least told me to compare several offers.*

Justin went to his next several classes and was finally finished with school by 1:50 p.m. He was beginning to think that today was just for making class announcements. At work, several students needed Justin's help to try to get their student computer accounts set up. Among several students who needed help, one asked, "What are those little red squiggles under the words on my essay in MS Word?" Justin had to hold back his laughter.

Applying for FAFSA

During a lull at work, Justin started working on an essay, but then he remembered that he had to go to www.fafsa.gov and complete his FAFSA. He went to the website and filled out the form. He knew how to answer most of the questions, but there were several questions he needed to ask his mom about. He quickly emailed his mom and then logged in to his social media account to see what his friends were up to.

Pling! Went Justin's chat window. There was a message was from Paul. "Dude, what's up? How were classes today?"

"Fine—kind of boring for most of them," Justin typed.

"Most?" Paul asked.

"Well, my first class of the day, the professor seems to be a real jerk," Justin replied.

"Ditch the class, if you can, and move on." Paul messaged. "Any cute girls?☺"

"Well, in the same class as that jerk of a professor, there was a really cute girl." Justin wrote back.

"What's her name?" Paul asked.

"Allison Pratt," Justin replied.

"Did you get her number?" Paul messaged.

"No," said Justin. "I only found out her name because the teacher was grilling several students."

"That's OK," Paul typed.

"Excuse me," said a student in the computer lab. Justin turned and saw a guy standing there.

"Got to go," Justin typed. "Work is calling." He closed the chat session with Paul. He asked the student, "What can I help you with?"

The student requested help with some formatting for a paper; Justin went over to assist.

Upon returning to his desk, he found another chat message was open. It was Justin's mom.

"Hi, sweetie. How were classes?"

Not wanting to worry her, Justin wrote, "Okay. It was mostly just going over the syllabi. Mom, did you get my e-mail?" Justin typed, not waiting for her to read the email.

"I haven't checked my e-mail yet. What was it about?" Justin's mom wrote back.

"A teacher is having us fill out a FAFSA application for an assignment."

"I've heard about those from a friend, but didn't know how to get them" said Justin's mother. "It's good you're filling it out, especially with Dad's income being what it is."

"Yeah, I guess so. I need to know if I am going to be claimed as a dependent for taxes and what Dad's income for last year was," Justin typed.

"For taxes, you can claim yourself; we won't list you as a dependent. I'll look at the income levels on our taxes."

"Thanks, Mom," Justin said.

"Have you found a place to stay?" his mom asked, obviously implying a place *not* with Dave and Susan.

"Not yet," Justin said. "There's an online website where people post rooms available, and there's also a student board where ads are posted."

"Well, don't wait too long," his mom said.

"Yeah, I know. Actually, the same teacher who gave me the assignment about the FAFSA told me to go to Student Housing, and I found out that the university requires students to live in places that are approved for student housing."

"It sounds like this teacher is teaching you a lot," Justin's mom replied.

"I guess so," Justin said.

"I'll check on Dad's income and answer your e-mail later today," his mom replied.

"Thanks, Mom," Justin said.

"Sure thing, I love you. Dad and I are praying for you."

"Thanks, Mom."

The chat session ended.

Justin decided to write that essay paper now and start his reading assignments. He got up a few times after writing two to three paragraphs to check on the students in the lab. After his paper was written, his brain felt like mush. He checked his e-mail. *No message from Mom yet. I'll go and at least fill out a profile at that Fastweb place. I may not have my FAFSA done, but maybe I can get around that.*

Scholarship Starts—What is Out There

He went to *www.fastweb.com* website and filled out a profile. There were questions about his parents, his religion, his hobbies, his major, where he had lived, his likes, and even some questions about his past schooling. In high school, he had had a 3.16 GPA and had gotten a score of 23 on the ACT. *Okay,* he thought to himself before clicking the final submit button, *I'll bet there are only three scholarships offered to me at this point. I mean, you've basically got to have a 4.0 and 30-something on the ACT to get a scholarship.* Justin hit "submit" and the Fastweb website indicated that there were 83 scholarships available to him.

"Whoa!" Justin said softly to himself. "I really don't believe this happened! Score!"

The website indicated that if he were to get all 83 scholarships available over the next year, he would have $187,418 available for his use. He clicked on the scholarship that had the soonest submission deadline. He read the scholarship description and then the requirements. It was for $2,000. Justin saw that one of the requirements was completing the FAFSA profile. *Okay, Professor Christensen, you've piqued my interest. Maybe you* do *know what you're talking about— we'll see.* Justin thought. He marked a few of the scholarships as his favorites, and then signed out of the site.

He did a final check of his e-mail with 15 minutes before his shift ended and found that his mom had replied with the information he needed for his FAFSA. Justin logged back on to his FAFSA profile, and quickly entered the information he had received from his mom. After hitting the submit button, he was shocked to see that he had been awarded a Federal Pell Grant for the amount of this semester's tuition plus $100 extra.[10] That was money that he didn't have to work for. *Maybe I don't need the student loan after all?* Justin mused.

Justin was excited. The Pell Grant was going to be sent to the Campus Tuition Department and not to Justin directly. He made a .pdf of the submission, indicating the amount. He quickly packed up his belongings and logged off the computer. Erin was going to be there soon, and it was time to go. Professor Christensen may be rigid, but he certainly knew what he was doing.

Justin went back to Dave's house, and started eating dinner. As Justin ate his food, he examined his ads for housing. He called on some and made appointments that night to go and see some of the places that sounded promising. After driving around to look at several nearby places, Justin finally visited one place that he particularly liked. He arranged to move in by the end of the week. Justin was glad to find a place.

Scholarship Essays and Applications 'Recycling'

The next day, he was at work in the computer lab. He found the final two ads for his housing assignment and submitted them. He also finished up the essay for another class. He logged back on to www. fastweb.com and looked again at the requirements for the scholarships he had liked. One of the scholarships required an essay that essentially was the same topic as the essay he had just written for his class. Justin looked at the paper he had written and wondered if it was good enough

---

10 FAFSA really takes 3-14 business days, but for the story's sake, it was instant. Plan ahead.

to submit. He contacted the student writing lab and set up an appointment to review his essay after work so that he could submit it as part of the scholarship. He also decided that he would at least meet with a scholarship counselor for his major's department and see if there were any scholarships available to him. And since he didn't have class tomorrow morning, he could meet then—before the financial counselor.

When Justin finished work, he went to the writing lab. The tutor reviewed Justin's essay and gave some tips on how to cite the sources a little better and improve the grammar. Justin edited and improved the paper, both for class and for the scholarship. *Awesome! Killing two birds with one stone!*

After work, Justin called some ads for housing. After looking at a few places, Justin found a house near the university. He would share a room with a guy named Nate.

At Dave and Susan's house that night, Justin asked to use the Internet, and he applied for the scholarship, submitting his essay. As he copied his essay from MS Word to the online form, he noticed, on Dave and Susan's desk a bill that was stamped "Overdue." Justin didn't pry, but he realized that his cousin was not doing as well financially as he had thought.

Dave came into the room and asked how Justin was.

"Things are going all right," Justin said, trying to act normal after seeing the bill.

"Whatcha up to?" Dave asked as he came in the room.

"Just workin' on some homework," Justin said.

"I'm telling you, man, you have got to take some fun classes, or you won't be able to enjoy your college time as much," Dave said with a friendly, reminding tone.

Remembering the bill he had seen, Justin replied, "Yeah, you're probably right... Hey– by the way, may I pay you something for the food and time spent here?" he offered.

"No, don't worry about it. Glad to help," Dave replied.

Justin wasn't so sure.

Scholarship Counselors in Your Major

The next morning, Justin met with a scholarship counselor from his major. The counselor was a man in his mid-forties who wanted to be called Bob. He looked over Justin's student profile on the computer screen.

"For freshmen, we have two scholarships you can apply for," Bob said. "One is for doing some research and then writing a paper—that one is for half tuition. The other scholarship is for $500, and you have to write a paper."

"What do I have to do to apply?" Justin asked.

"You'll need to..." Bob started reading off the scholarship requirements. "Why don't I just print these off for you, instead?"

He handed the pages to Justin. "You'll need to hurry to submit those," Bob said. "The deadline for the $500 one is Monday. You can e-mail me the completed applications."

Justin thanked Bob and put the papers away.

"Be sure to come back when you're a sophomore. There's a full-tuition scholarship that our department offers. By the way, have you tried the Campus Scholarship Department? They have a lot of scholarships that are available to students. There's money that goes unclaimed every year and just goes back into the fund, so you should definitely apply there," Bob stated as he looked at Justin.

"Where are they located?" Justin asked.

"They're in the Student Center on the third floor. In fact, I have access to their calendars. Let me check when someone is available to talk to you," Bob said as he turned back to his computer. "There's a slot available in 10 minutes; if you hurry, you can make it. Would you like to take it?"

"Sure," Justin replied. He figured that since this appointment had been brief, he might as well take the opportunity to see what the Campus Scholarship Department had to offer.

At the Campus Scholarship Department, Justin was sent by the department secretary to the office of the counselor Bob had arranged for him to meet, a man named Mr. Wheatley. The scholarship counselor asked Justin some questions. After he was finished, Mr. Wheatley said, "Hey, good news! Your father's employment has a scholarship fund here at the school. All incoming freshmen get a $120 scholarship to buy books."

"What if I already bought my books?" Justin asked hopefully, remembering how Paul had helped him earlier, and trying not to wonder if his dad's company had enough money to pay the bill.

"You can pocket the money if you submit your receipts," the Mr. Wheatley said.

"What do I have to do?" Justin asked.

"Just tell me at which branch your father works at and his full name, so that they can track it down."

Justin told him the information, and Mr. Wheatley submitted it. "Okay, it looks like this will be verified and then credited to your student account in about a week. When it's there, you can go to the cashier's office and get a check from them. You're also invited to apply to the general scholarship fund. The university offers full, half, and quarter scholarships from this fund. There are more scholarships available later for sophomores, juniors, and seniors. As a note, there are additional scholarships if you join an honor society or club."

"How do I apply?" Justin asked.

"You fill out an application on our website and then get a teacher recommendation," Mr. Wheatley responded. "The teacher can send the letter of recommendation in for you to the e-mail address listed here." He pointed to the e-mail address on the website. "Don't worry—you can find us on the university website, searching for scholarships. However, you do need to have this done by Monday, to meet the deadline."

"Why Monday?" Justin asked.

"It's the Add/Drop deadline, and scholarships must be accounted for by this time. Think of it as an airplane standby. If there's a seat available, you may get a ride or be changed to another flight, but if you don't at least submit a request with a standby ticket, you won't get to fly on the plane, even if there *is* a vacant seat. Scholarships work the same way. If there is one available, you may get it; but if you don't at least apply, then you won't get it, even if there *is* one that could work for you." Mr. Wheatley responded as if he had had that example prepared in advance.

Justin thanked him and then left the room, feeling a little bit more gleeful. He had just received $120 because of his father's work, and all he'd had to do was spend fifteen minutes with a counselor!

Justin decided that he was going to spend all of his time at work applying to scholarships that had deadlines within the next two weeks. The counselor was right: he may not get every scholarship he applied to, but at least by applying, he improved his chances of getting some cash.

The only teacher who even took note of Justin was Mr. Christensen. *Since I'm a freshman, who else but Professor Christensen would write me a letter of recommendation? But he'd probably scoff at my request for help,* Justin thought to himself. He didn't have time to ask another teacher—it was Friday, the assignment was due Saturday, and the deadline for all the scholarships was Monday. Justin stopped at a computer kiosk and wrote a quick e-mail. He decided the positive approach might be best for someone as grumpy as the professor.

> *Dear Professor Christensen,*
>
> *You may not believe this, but I've done most of what you said. I applied to the FAFSA and received tuition + $100. I received a book scholarship from my dad's work for $120. And I was able to get some great advice on what to avoid with student housing by talking to the housing department. Thanks to your assignment, I found a really good deal—and close to campus—that I am renting for a modest price.[11]*
>
> *I want to apply to the campus general scholarship as another scholarship to apply for and I need a letter of recommendation from a teacher. I am a freshman, and since you are the only teacher who even knows who I am, I am asking you. (Just as a reminder, you spoke with me after class on Wednesday and said that you wanted me to take the class.) I am asking if you'd send a letter of recommendation to the Scholarship Department on my behalf. It needs to be received by Monday. I can submit my scholarship application prior to that, and the department staff will wait for*

---

11 For this assignment, see *Winning the Money Game in College: Real Estate.*

your letter to arrive. I will submit my part of the application this afternoon.

Justin then provided the professor with the Scholarship Department's e-mail address, his student number, and copied the information from the website about the scholarship, and closed his note with his own contact information.

Justin hoped that Professor Christensen would be empathetic and write a nice letter of recommendation for him. *Well, even if he blows me off, I'm really no worse off than I am now.*

Justin was hungry, but he decided to go to the Student Ad Board in the Student Center to get information about the rooms for rent available. He went to the Student Center and, after asking some students for directions, found the ad board. There were jobs, computers, and rooms-for-rent posted on index cards. Justin took several of the rental ads for his assignment. As Justin was passing the student food court in the Student Center, he saw Allison, the girl from his finance class, working at one of the food vendors. Justin decided to go buy some food at her station.

"Hey, aren't you in that personal finance class?" Allison asked Justin.

"Yeah, I think so," Justin said, trying not to sound as if he had paid much attention to her in class.

"What do you think of our professor?" Allison asked.

"He seems a little rough around the edges, but I was already able to get the cost of tuition plus $100 by filling out my FAFSA, plus I got a $120 scholarship because of my dad's work."

"Good for you!" Allison said. "What did you do to get the scholarship?"

"Spend 15 minutes, and answer some questions, with the school scholarship counselor. I only met with the counselor simply because I was trying to fulfill Professor Christensen's assignment to apply to scholarships," Justin replied.

"You got $120 for 15 minutes, plus all of tuition covered with your FAFSA just because you were following the professor's assignment?!" Allison asked incredulously.

"Well, yes, and he did kind of help me with housing, but I just don't want to be challenged on every point with his 'my rules, my class, there's the door' attitude," Justin replied.

"Your total is $8.41," Allison said. She looked pensive.

"Ouch," said Justin. "You don't happen to have any discounts or coupons circulating?" Justin asked hopefully, remembering his experience with the tire.

"We do have a coupon with Groupon if you happen to have one of those," Allison said consolingly.

"What's Groupon?"

"Groupon.com is a website that has deals for dining, travel, and services. Merchants want to be advertised, and they post deals—generally for half off or better."

"Sounds cool." Justin pulled out his smartphone and purchased a coupon. He then showed the coupon to Allison.

"Wait," said Allison. "This coupon is for $5.00 off an order of $10.00 or more. I won't be able to accept it unless you spend another $1.90—not counting the tax."

"Well, in that case, give me some fresh-baked bread for $2.00," Justin said.

"Your new total is $5.48," Allison said with a smile.

As Justin paid, he asked, "So are you going to take the personal finance class?"

"I don't know," said Allison. "The course seemed good, but the professor was too much 'in your face.' By the way, what did he say to you after class?" Allison asked curiously.

"He just told me two things. One: he liked me for standing up for that guy in our class, and he wants me to take the class, and, two: something about things not always being what they seem and that in order to get gold, I need to do things that most people don't know how to, or where to look—or something like that," Justin responded.

"Hmmm," said Allison. "Have you found any gold?" she asked with a smile.

"Not unless you count the student housing and the FAFSA money and scholarship," Justin responded.

"Maybe," said Allison. "Take care."

"You, too," said Justin as the next customer took his spot in line at the cashier. Justin sat at a table and ate his food. *She was nice,* he thought, and then he realized she never said she would be taking the class. *She's a tricky one.*

Justin had to rush to his next class. At 1 p.m. he had only 30 minutes including travel time to meet with the financial counselor.

School Financial Counselors—May Help Find Options

Justin met with the counselor, Frank Walters, a few minutes after his appointment.

"I'd like to know about getting a student loan."

"Have you applied to the FAFSA, the Free Application for Federal Student Aid?" Mr. Walters asked.

"Yes, I was awarded tuition plus $100."

"Do you have any scholarships?"

"Just one for $120 for books," Justin answered.

"Have you applied to any other scholarships?"

"Yes, I applied to one scholarship, soon to complete two more by Saturday. One was with my major, one from Fastweb, and the last being the general scholarship on campus."

"Are you married or the father of any children?"

"No."

"Are you presently employed, and if so, how many hours per week are you working?"

"I have a job as a lab aid. I'm working 15–20 hours."

"Do you have any other debts, such as credit cards?"

"No."

"Are your parents claiming you as a dependent, or are you being helped with tuition by them in any way?"

"No to both questions."

"Look, a lot of students think that they need a student loan because that's what everyone else is doing, but by the sounds of things, you already have tuition covered and a job. While true that your parents may not be helping you, you seem to already have your expenses covered. I would have pointed you to first apply to FAFSA, check with your department and the campus scholarship fund, and consider getting a student job—but you have already done all of that. I can't tell you what to do with a loan, but really, why do you need it?"

Justin thought about it for a moment. It kind of surprised him that the counselor wasn't trying to sell him any student loans.[12] The nagging pit in his gut that had accompanied Justin for days since the news from his mom was gone.

"You can always come back next semester and apply for a student loan," Mr. Walters said, "but if you don't get a student loan this semester, you can save yourself one extra semester of future payments that you don't need. Some students say that they need a loan, but many of them are just too scared or lazy to go and get a job to pay for school or rent. You are one of the most ready students I have seen as a freshman; if you keep applying to more scholarships you will be fine. Who taught you to do all of this?"

"A lot of people have helped, plus a teacher required some of it as an assignment."

"You should thank that teacher, student loans can be helpful, but they can also hurt your financial future."

Justin thanked Mr. Walters and then ran to class.

Basic Tips for Writing Essays

Justin spent the rest of the day attending classes and then going to work and doing some readings for homework. When he got a moment, he decided to apply for the general campus scholarship; this scholarship had one of the nearest deadlines. The application on the website

---

12 This may not be the case with all counselors.

turned out to be a very lengthy one. Justin was asked to write three 250- to 400-word essays, one on each of the following topics: his leadership abilities, why he needs a scholarship, and someone who has inspired him.

Justin knew the dangers of typing into a browser form; he'd lost many a paper because of an online glitch. Instead, he typed his essays into MS Word and copied and pasted them onto the scholarship application. Thankfully, the lab was really slow after 3:30 p.m. *After all,* Justin thought, *it is Friday.*

The scholarship application took him about an hour, but he finally finished and submitted it. He saved a screen shot and submitted it on the class website. He went to his e-mail account and composed an e-mail to Professor Christensen, attaching the screen shot (of his confirmation) to the original e-mail he had sent earlier and then added, "I just submitted my application. In an effort to fulfill the requirements, I need a letter of recommendation from a teacher." Justin sent the e-mail.

He then decided to write the 500-word essay for the scholarship from his department, just in case Professor Christensen didn't respond favorably to his request for help, or in case the professor discredited Justin's effort because of "not doing all of the requirements." Justin could see Professor Christensen taunting him for that very reason.

Justin took out the pages Bob had given him. The topic was Why I Chose My Major. *Well, if I get the scholarship,* Justin mused, *that's a dollar per word.* He wanted the scholarship over with, so he typed quickly and did a spell check. Upon finishing, he submitted his essay, saved a screenshot of the confirmation, and submitted the screenshot to the class website.

"Done!" Justin said to himself. He was glad it was Friday and hoped to get a little break from homework. He looked for events going on at campus later tonight.

Chapter 4: Principles and Suggestions

1. Apply to FAFSA first because many scholarships require that you submit an application to FAFSA before applying for their scholarships.

    a. Go to www.fafsa.gov fill out an application.

    b. The FAFSA takes 3-10 business days to process.

    c. If you attended the year before but did not apply to a FAFSA grant, you can back-date the application for usually one year if you were in school. Check the website for more details.

    d. Other grants may be available for you depending on availability and your major.

2. Apply to as many scholarships as you can. Scholarships can stack, meaning that once tuition has been covered, you may get to keep the remaining money as long as you abide by the parameters of your scholarship(s). If you don't apply, you cannot get the scholarships. Go to *www.CollegeCashChampion.com* and see the videos on how to apply to scholarships and scholarship sequences.

    a. Apply to one to two scholarships every week.

    b. Start by filling out an application and profile at www.fastweb.com and/or https://bigfuture.collegeboard.org/scholarship-search.

    c. Check with your major's department for scholarships.

    d. Check with the campus scholarship department for scholarships.

    e. Save your essays, submission requirements, project descriptions/reports, and any submitted materials.

        i. Often essays you do for classes can be submitted for scholarships.

        ii. Many times you can reuse your same essays, etc. for different scholarships—always check the scholarship rules.

    f. Go to the campus writing center and ask for help in reviewing your essays.

    g. You don't have to be perfect to receive scholarships, but you do have to submit applications.

h. Sometimes you can get a teacher to alter an assignment if you ask politely and indicate that you would like to write an essay (or do a project) on a topic that not only has some relevance to the class, but can also be used to apply for a scholarship. Ask if you can substitute an assignment.

i. If a scholarship ever comes up in your department, apply. Often there are very few students who apply.

- Years ago, the author of this book was made aware of a really prestigious scholarship in his major, but failed to apply, thinking that there would probably be 50 other applicants. However, there were only three applicants, and the two who won were less academically qualified than the author. Apply for every department scholarship.

- Another time, the author of this book was given a full-ride scholarship for three years from his department simply for writing a 200- to 500-word essay. The author was awarded the scholarship by a teacher who knew the author. It pays to apply to department scholarships.

3. If you have the ability, apply for 20 to 50 scholarships over the semester. That quantity may be boring, but it will help you get the best possible results. ***Which would you rather do: spend a hundred hours applying to scholarships, or 20 years paying off student loans?*** You may need to contact your department, the campus scholarship department or your high school (if you are a college freshman), etc.

a. (See *www.CollegeCashChampion.com* for a video on scholarship sequencing.)

b. The advantage in doing this early is that as the semester continues, you will get busier. Take the time to do it now.

c. Keep your essays and application materials in a folder on your computer and in an online location, such as on a web drive or your email. You can re-use many of your essays for future scholarships.

    d.   When given an assignment in school that involves an essay, a project, public speaking, or other assignment, find out if you can turn this into a scholarship application. This will allow you to kill two birds with one stone.

4.   Willingness to take just a few extra steps can make a big difference. If there is something that allows you a big payoff, using honorable means, then by all means, do it. You will be no worse off if you don't get it than you are now, but if you *do* get it, you will be a lot better off. By all means, try.

5.   Use essays repeatedly for assignments and essay portions of scholarships.

Chapter 4: Warning and Avoidance

1.   Justin earned money, and then treated himself with food. It is good to celebrate the victories—just keep them in balance. The point is to do more than just break-even; it is to grow your money.

2.   Student loans are permanent. Right now, unless legislation changes, even if you declare bankruptcy, get medically ill, or otherwise cannot pay, the loans are NOT going away. They are VERY financially binding.

3.   FAFSA will take longer for your application to be approved than it did in the story. Keep in mind that it takes 3-10 business days.

4.   Don't apply for a student loan if you don't need it. You are just costing yourself money.

Chapter 5: Truths Unveiled

Justin got up Saturday morning and read, and then he went for a run. Upon coming back home, Justin found Dave in the kitchen in his pajamas. He grinned and announced, "So today's the big moving day, huh?!"

"Yeah," Justin said, "I'll be calling the guys at the house a little bit later, and then I'll move my stuff over."

Justin and Dave chatted a bit more before he packed up his stuff. He figured that 10 a.m. would be a good time to call the guys at his new place.

"Um, could you come at 4:00 today?" asked Nate, Justin's new roommate. "A bunch of us are going mountain biking mid-day."

"I guess that would work," Justin said.

Later that day, Justin moved in. About 7:30 p.m. he was still getting situated. Nate came in and said, "So, do you go to church?"

Justin responded in the affirmative, and Nate said, "Great! Church is at 11:00 a.m. This week the lesson is on service."

At the mention of *service*, Justin remembered his third assignment that he had meant to do earlier: he needed to create a plan of where he wanted to give 10% of his income and how he would give five hours of service each week. And he needed to have the plan submitted before 8 p.m.

"Real quick," Justin said, "I just remembered that I need to get on the Internet and submit an assignment before 8 p.m. to have it count." He had a mental image of Professor Christensen throwing him out of his class for not finishing his last assignment.

Giving 10% was not really that hard. Justin had long since been taught the importance of tithing his church. The service part of the assignment was a bit harder, since he didn't know where he could serve. Justin pulled up the class website on his laptop and found that he could count some of his time at church toward service, if he helped out at church. He still needed to come up with about three hours more. He continued reading on the website and learned that he could get credit for greeting 10 people each week with a sincere smile and asking with interest how they were doing—but this only gave him 30 more minutes. He needed three more hours.

Justin consulted his roommates. "Hey, I'm trying to do an assignment, and I need to have three hours of service per week; does anyone have some ideas?"

His roommates suggested: "Why don't you come and sing with us at an old folks' home? We do that every Sunday." "How about volunteering at the University Service Center?" "Maybe tutor someone?"

Justin decided that he would write down: singing at the old folks' home and volunteering at the University Service Center. He put his plan together, along with the mention of tithing, and hit "submit." The time was 7:56 p.m. He had made it! Now, all he had to do was show up at class at 7 a.m. Monday morning. That was a lot of work just to get accepted into a class. It better be worth it! He felt sure though. He was going to get a lot out of the class based on what he'd already learned from these assignments.

A New Day—A Metaphor for Change

On Monday, Justin arrived at the classroom at 6:55 a.m. As he walked in, he saw some students leaving the room, in a hurry. He went into the classroom and read on the chalkboard:

Class location has been changed to the Jones Building, room 455. This is also in your e-mail, sent this morning at 6:30 a.m. You must be in the room in the Jones Building by no later than 7:05 a.m. Please note the camera, which is to make sure that you did, in fact, come by 7 a.m.

–Professor Christensen

P.S. Take a map with you and an assignment page.

Stationed above the chalkboard was a circular camera that Justin had not noticed before. He checked his e-mail on his Smartphone to make sure this was not a joke and, sure enough, Professor Christensen's message was there. On the table below the chalkboard was a stack of campus maps, as well pieces of paper with blanks on them, as if for a game of Hangman.

— — — — — — — — — — — — — — —

Justin now understood why the other students were in a hurry. He picked up a map and a pink sheet of paper and started a fast-paced walk to the Jones Building, the next building over. When he got inside the Jones Building, he ran up the four flights of stairs and entered the appointed classroom at 7:02. He saw written on the chalkboard:

The fourth letter of the first word is "A." Meet us for class at the Smith Building, at the plaque in the northeast entrance. You have till 7:09 a.m. to get there.

I was just at *the Smith Building*. Justin marked his paper:

— — — A — — — — — — — — — — —

When Justin arrived at the location, he read the words engraved on the stone plaque: "Our Heritage Is to Move Forward Boldly in Our Cause. –Albert H. Smith" Attached to the plaque, on bright pink paper, was a note which read:

The second letter of the second word is the last letter of the phrase on your paper. You need to go to Jones Building, room 102. You must be there by 7:14 a.m. Please note the camera.

Justin looked up and saw a security camera positioned right at the plaque. *Why can't we just get all of the letters at the same building?* Justin thought to himself. He marked his paper and then headed off.

— — — A — — — — — — — — — — E

Justin kept on getting directed to go to and from the Jones and Smith Buildings—back and forth. One time he went to a vending machine, another time to a campus statue, and another time to a janitor closet. Each time, Justin had to cross between the two buildings. He was getting tired of just going back and forth to the buildings. When he went to one building, he briefly looked around and tried to see any other clues, but they were too well hidden.

His paper now read:

__ __ C_ A_ __ E_ _____ __ A_ __ R_ A_ __ E_

He was on his way to the Smith Building, and he had to be there by 7:39. He had saved some time by running, and it was now 7:30. He began to wonder if Professor Christensen was really watching the cameras, or if the students were making fools of themselves going back and forth.

His next few letters came, and he had:

E_ __ C_ A_ __ E_ _____ __ A_ T_ R_ A_ __ E_

Justin didn't really have time to guess at the missing letters. The times were getting shorter now, and he had to go to the locations anyway to get the next letter.

After a few more letters, he had:

E_ __ C_ A_ P_ E_ _____ R_ A_ T_ R_ A_ C_
                    _E_

He figured out the words "escape" and "rat race," and he guessed at possibilities for the middle word, such as "my," or "this," or even "the," but he needed to keep going between the Smith and Jones Buildings. He had shaved about 15 minutes off his time. Justin then saw a guy with a paper similar to his, who stopped him.

"Hey, I don't know where the fountain is that Professor Christensen was talking about," the guy said.

The fountain was two clues back. Justin wondered if he should help this guy, or not. After all, Justin had found out these letters *himself*. He then remembered the rule, "When asked for help, we help."

"The fountain is around the corner, and off to the left," Justin said with a smile. "You'll still need to show up, as there's a camera on the fountain."

"Thanks," said the guy, and he took off running, as did Justin—but in the opposite direction.

Justin found the "S" in escape at the next clue. He then found the word "the" at the next clue. Finally, Justin came to a room that had a note written on the blackboard: "Look at the answer sheet sideways." Justin turned his assignment sheet on the side and towards the bottom, in a small font, he was directed to an upper room that was part of the Smith Building; he had to be there by 8:29. He had plenty of time to arrive, as it was only 7:55 a.m.

Escaping the Rat Race

At the door, stood Professor Christensen with a smile on his face. He greeted Justin warmly and said: "Mr. Murray, I'm so glad to see you. You obviously learned that things are not always as they seem. Come on in and have some bagels, cream cheese, and orange juice. You might like the show, as well. By the way, how did you like the rat race—showing up at times required by someone else, always going back and forth, and trying to 'keep up with the Jones'?"

"It was kind of frustrating, and felt like I was wasting my time, just going back and forth, and when I finally got to the end and found that I could have accomplished the same thing with less time and effort, I was annoyed." Justin said.

"I agree. Here's a dollar for your time," Professor Christensen said as he handed Justin a dollar.

Justin looked at the dollar and felt it really wasn't worth his time and effort. He entered the room and saw several students, many of whom he didn't recognize from the first day of class. Also, some of the students from the first day were not present—they apparently had decided not to take the class. There was a projector displaying scenes on a screen with eight split screens and a clock in the bottom corner of each section. On the screens, Justin saw the original classroom, the fountain, the plaque, and several other locations. He watched as his fellow students were running back and forth.

Justin then saw Allison. She was here! Justin was secretly happy. He looked at the table by her and saw that there were whole-wheat bagels, cream cheese, and bottles of orange juice. He headed over; she was eating a bagel.

"How's it going?" Allison asked him.

"Okay. How did you beat me here?" Justin asked with a smile, grabbing a bagel.

"I saw Professor Christensen's e-mail, and started before you did," Allison responded. "I noticed the small print when I stopped to tie my shoe... Professor Christensen did a good job making the clues go in a circle, so that students couldn't find the other clues. It was kind of funny and sad to watch everyone run the rat race. Thanks for the tip the other day. I was questioning whether I wanted to be in this class, but when I heard your results, and the tip about looking for gold, I figured I should at least try. It turns out that Professor Christensen wasn't what he seemed at first, either. He seems really nice."

"It surprised me, when I came in, how friendly he was. What did you think of his rat race?" Justin asked.

"It seemed a lot like my job, a lot of effort and little pay," Allison said. This got Justin thinking about work and how he seemed to be going back and forth—always on someone else's schedule. "Hey– that rude guy is coming in," Allison said as she pointed towards the screen.

Justin turned and saw the guy (who had argued with Professor Christensen during the first class) on the screen, coming up to the room. Justin looked at the clock and saw that it was 8:27 a.m. The spikey-haired guy came in with a scowl on his face.

Professor Christensen closed the door to the room and announced, "Everyone who would like me to sign an Add/Drop card may come up front, and we'll get those signed so that you can take off. All that will be left is for you go to the Registrar's Office and drop off the card.

"What was it like going back and forth between the Smith and Jones buildings?" Professor Christensen asked.

"Awful."

"I felt like I was getting nowhere,"

"I was annoyed, until I saw the answer written on the side of the sheet, then I realized it was a game you were playing."

"I thought it was ridiculous."

"This is how life often expects us to live our lives. Going here, there, and everywhere on other people's schedules," Professor Christensen said. "I want to teach you all how to live your life in a way that you choose what you do with your time. Sometimes it is necessary to run the rat race, until you learn how to escape, but try to make it a minimum."

"T. Harv Eker in his book *Your Millionaire Mind* tells how in his mid-twenties, he wanted to go into the pie business, but didn't know that much about that industry. He got a job as a pie shelf stocker and learned the business; he learned about the suppliers, the customers, the products, and ultimately, he learned that he didn't want to be in the pie business. He realized that this type of work was not fulfilling to him. Conveniently, he was paid to come to this realization."

"A few days after he quit, he was asked by a former co-worker about going into another business in the fitness industry. He also investigated this industry and found it to be an emerging opportunity. He really enjoyed this line of work and this opportunity led to a new career path for him, and ultimately made him a millionaire. T. Harv Eker was in the rat race to learn how to get out. Sometimes it is necessary to be in the rat race, but only as you are looking for ideas or gaining capital. We will talk more about practical steps on how to get out of the race later in the semester. Just like the race I had you all participate in today, all of you carried the answers with you, but you didn't know it. You can achieve the same results a lot quicker if you just learn how and where to look."

"If you learn to do things just a little differently, you can have and do things that other people only dream of. You don't have to be *ten* times better, just a *little* bit better. In the Olympics, the first-, second-, third-, and fourth-place winners could all finish within half a second of each other. Now, the first-place winner is not 10 times better—just a few milliseconds better, but gets roughly 10 times the amount of fame that the second-place winner gets because book authors, talk shows, and company sponsors line up to interview and reward this individual. In turn, the second-place winner gets about 10 times more reward than the third-place winner. As for the fourth-place winner, he or she might get an article written in the local, hometown newspaper, along with some local and fleeting fame, but that doesn't equal the reward of the first-place winner for just being a little bit better. That is all it takes, not a huge amount of effort, just a little bit of directed effort. Later in the semester, I am going to teach you some business concepts that, if you apply, may allow you never to have to enter the rat race and to choose to be free to live your life."[13]

Professor Christensen continued, "I want you all to know that who I was *pretending* to be last class and who I *really* am are completely different. In fact, when Mr. Murray, here called me on my ploy, I had a hard time keeping a straight face and not laughing. As an apology for acting like a jerk, we are going bowling for the next class—completely free to you, if you get to the campus lanes in the Student Center by 7 a.m. on Wednesday; otherwise, you will pay $12 for the lane, the shoes, and a late fee."

There were expressions of excitement.

"One last thing– pick up the two handouts by the door on your way out. They will help you with your scholarship assignments. One is en-titled '*How to Apply to Scholarships in Under an Hour*' and the other is called '*Scholarship Application Sequence.*'[14] These two handouts will prove to be very valuable to you in applying for scholarships."

Cash Strapped—Planning in Advance

Justin went to the office to turn in his 'Add/Drop' card. There was a line, but Justin wanted to wait to get this class—plus he was going bowling. While Justin waited he started thinking. *Well, I was certainly wrong about Professor Christensen. I guess that was why his face was twitching the other day: he was trying not to laugh. I'm surprised I didn't realize it. Things are* not *always what they seem, and to find gold, I have to be willing to do what other people aren't willing to do.*

When he got to the office window a female student attendant took his Add/Drop card. "It looks like you have enough credits to be a full-time student status. Today is the deadline to pay tuition." She gave the cost of tuition.

"Did my Pell Grant come in?"

"It looks like your tuition has been covered. You are all set for this semester."

"Great!" Justin said, then turned and left.

---

13 For more information on this see: *Winning the Money Game in College: Business* by the author.

14 These two handouts are available at *www.CollegeCashChampion.com*.

His other classes went well; each was giving him more readings and homework. Justin wondered how he was going to do all that he was being asked. He raced home to grab some lunch between class and work and was handed some mail by one of his roommates. He stuffed the mail in his backpack, quickly grabbed a PB&J sandwich, and ran to work.

After helping a couple of students at his job, he opened up his mail. The first letter was from the University Scholarship Department. He was excited all over again! Justin opened the envelope and read the letter:

Dear Mr. Murray,

Thank you for applying to the campus general scholarship. We regret to inform you that you were not selected for the general scholarship for incoming freshman.

Best of luck to you. We encourage you to apply next year.

Sincerely,

Syracuse State University Scholarship Department

Justin was disappointed. *That stinks!* Justin thought. *I spent about 3 hours on that essay plus the revision time. I was kind of hoping to get at least a $100 scholarship. What kind of result is that?* Justin was a little miffed. He started thinking that he wasted his time. *What a waste! What good does applying to scholarships do if I can't even get one?* Justin was a little upset. The next letter was from his cell phone provider. Justin knew that that letter had been forwarded from his mom: it was his monthly bill. He put the rest of his mail aside and looked at his bank account.

Justin had not yet been paid from his job, and from the nearly $1,000 with which he had started, he paid off his credit card. Between the deposit for his rent, the monthly rent due, the new tire, books, gasoline, and food, he was down to $108.13.

Justin cringed. While true, he didn't have to pay tuition because of the Pell Grant, he was essentially broke. He wouldn't have much money left: the cell phone bill would be about $85, he wouldn't get his first check for two weeks—one more week of work, and another of processing. *How am I going to live for two weeks on about $10?* Justin didn't have an answer. *Maybe the student loan is needed.*

Justin was too upset to do any homework. He decided to check his email. There were a few emails, promotions, and one from Syracuse State University, with the subject "Urgent Attention Requested." Justin clicked on the email; it read:

Dear Mr. Murray,

The school has received your application for a Pell Grant. While you have been approved; however, there has been a delay in the release date from the government. Because of this year's early Add/Drop deadline, the funds will not be received till after the school starts.

You will still need to pay your tuition in full by the Add/Drop deadline. If you need a temporary loan, please see the tuition office prior to the Add/Drop deadline. Students who fail to pay for tuition prior to the Add/Drop deadline, whether through a loan or direct payment, will be discontinued from taking classes this semester.[15]

Sincerely,

Syracuse State University Department of Finance

Panic ensued Justin's mind. *The office will close in 6 minutes; there is no way I can make it there by 5 p.m. to pay for tuition and get a loan. Am I going to be dropped as a student? Why did the representative tell me my tuition had been covered when it really hadn't? Could I petition for an extension?*

Justin felt alone and for one of the first times in his life, he was scared of what finances could do to his future. The prerequisite classes for freshmen in his major were only offered in the fall. While he could take alternate classes next semester, he would still have to wait to take his major's prerequisites till next fall. All Justin could do was pray: *I need help. I need a miracle. Please help me find a way to pay for school.*

Justin didn't know what to do. He just felt sick. He quickly locked his computer, and decided that he would try to run to the tuition office to plead his case. As he got up, he noticed his pile of mail and below

---

15 This scenario is made up. Check with your school about processes.

his credit card bill there were several other letters. One was a junk mail offer for a credit card. At the bottom of the pile he saw a cream colored envelope. Justin grabbed his mail to shove into his bag, but stopped when he saw the cream colored envelope's return address: the Office of Prestigious Scholarships. Justin opened the envelope as he was half running down the hall.

The letter began with "Congratulations!" He had been awarded a full-tuition scholarship as long as he maintained a 3.5 GPA, starting this semester! It was called the Gordon and Betty Osborn Scholarship, given only to incoming freshman.

Justin was astounded. *Holy cow!* He couldn't believe it. He had just gotten a scholarship and not just any scholarship—a prestigious one! Justin moved up and down with enthusiasm; not really jumping, but almost.

Thank you God! Thank you! Thank you!

Justin hadn't been this ecstatic for a long time. He felt like he had as a kid when he got a bicycle that he wanted at Christmas.

Even though Justin was part way down the hall, he suddenly had an idea. *Maybe that is what the registrar's office lady meant about my tuition being covered.* Justin returned to the computer lab from where he had just rushed out. Some of the students looked at him with a weird, inquisitive look on their faces.

Justin quickly logged into his computer, then to the student portal, and went to the tuition payments. Tuition had been covered by the scholarship. The Pell grant was shown as pending. He also saw the $120 from his dad's work.

Because of the Pell grant and two scholarships, thousands of dollars were now at his disposal. Justin couldn't help thinking, *I'm rich! I wonder if I will get both.* Having two times the amount of tuition would be a great thing—plus he didn't have to work for this money.

Money Seeds—Paying it Forward

Wednesday came and Justin really enjoyed bowling with the class. He got a 147 and "just happened" to be on Allison's team. After bowling, the class went to the bowling center lobby. Professor Christensen had reserved the entire bowling alley for the class at hours not generally available to most students. At 7 a.m., the alley was usually closed.

Professor Christensen addressed the class. "Did you know that Jeff Olson, in his book, *The Slight Edge*, stated that the average millionaire's bowling score is under a hundred? His point was that you should focus on what gives you and your life freedom—that is, becoming a millionaire, instead of focusing exclusively on things that have little return in value, such as bowling. Focus on what matters to you, and let the rest be as it is. If your goal is to be a professional bowler, do that and be the best you can be. However, if your goal is to be wealthy, then focus on integrity and correct principles of building wealth, and let the unimportant stuff fall away."

A guy Justin hadn't met raised his hand and asked "Are you trying to tell us to not sweat the small things?"

"Exactly! Focus on what really matters to you."

"Class, you don't need to eliminate all fun and social events, but unless your goal is to become a professional bowler or a bowling instructor, you shouldn't put the time and energy into tasks that offer little reward. Don't worry if you don't do too well at insignificant things. Focus on what it is you truly want for yourself. Have fun as you attend college; however, by doing things just slightly differently than most people, you can have 10 times the rewards that they have." With a smile, the professor added, "By focusing on building wealth, you can *first* achieve financial independence and *then* go bowling— or whatever you wish, without the worries of meeting the day-to-day obligations that most people are faced with, day in and day out, and especially without the debt."

Justin realized the point of going bowling: *By focusing on what matters most, people can have, do, and be more than they otherwise could. He didn't need to eliminate fun, just choose what was important to him and focus on that.*

"Now, this being said," Professor Christensen again interrupted Justin's thoughts, using a compelling voice that brought attention back in, "even if you chose bowling as your medium, I can show you how you can do more with bowling than you had ever thought possible and make yourself wealthy in the process, but it requires you to do things in a new way that most people don't think to do. There are infinite ways to make money and become a millionaire, but if you follow a few key principles, getting wealth will be a lot easier and faster."

Justin could tell that Professor Christensen was really passionate about what he was teaching.

"Let me share an analogy that might help you," said the professor. "Let's imagine that in the Philippines there's a massive hurricane that wipes out all of the crops in early spring. Two Americans go over to help as volunteers: one is from a major city and has never been to a farm, and the other is from the country. As the Philippine lands are salvaged, some bags of rice are found that are unspoiled and intact. The country volunteer takes 10 percent of the bags and, with the help of the people, starts planting the rice in the ground. Now, the city volunteer would question the sanity of the other volunteer. 'What are you doing?' the city volunteer says. 'These people *need* this rice; they're starving. Why are you just wasting it, throwing it into the ground?' The country volunteer says, 'I know. That's why I'm planting it now. The only way to increase what they have in the future is to *plant* this rice. For every grain that is planted, at least 20 to 300 more grains will grow from it. By putting at least 10% of this rice into the ground, we're providing for the people *so* much more rice than the 10% we're planting.'"

Professor Christensen then asked the class, "Who do you think was doing more to help the people living with the destruction from the hurricane: the volunteer from the city or the one from the country?"

"The one from the country," a girl responded.

"Why?" Professor Christensen asked her and the class.

"Well," the girl began, "the guy from the country is giving the people more food and more grain by planting it. He is helping them to rebuild."

"Do you think that to the inexperienced volunteer from the city, the actions seem foolish—I mean, putting stuff in the ground, expecting it to grow?" Professor Christensen asked.

"I suppose so," said another guy in the class, "but that's only because he hasn't seen stuff grow before and has no experience with harvesting crops."

"Very good," said Professor Christensen.

"Wait, that's messed up," said the spikey-haired guy. "Why couldn't the people in the story have eaten their rice and waited for other countries to help them out? I mean, they're obviously sending two Americans, why couldn't they have planted the rice and seeds sent from other countries, instead of their own rice? They'd still get crops at the end of the harvest."

"Interesting point, Mr. Fredrickson," said Professor Christensen.

"It's Malcolm," he responded curtly.

"All right, Malcolm, let's look at it. First, they don't know how long other countries will continue to support them, especially if they don't try to support themselves when they have the means. Second, they'll still have to plant something in order to continue to eat, and since those crops take time to grow, if the people wait longer to plant they may not have fully-developed rice when they need it."

"*Whatever*! I'd still eat the bags of rice while I had them," Malcolm said "what good is future rice if everyone is dead?"

"It sounds to me as though you can relate more to the volunteer from the city than the one from the country," Professor Christensen said politely to the comment. "I want to come to you as an experienced, old farmer who knows how to grow *money*. Money seeds act the same way as the rice in this story, and we need to plant them. How we plant them is by taking 10% of our money and giving it to worthy causes in the form of tithing. Just like planting crops, money crops require seeds. When you plant corn, you first have to 'give away' some of your corn by planting it, but in return at the harvest you get hundreds of corn kernels returned to you. I can tell you from my experience: tithing works."

"Let's consider the facts and evidences. Many of the wealthiest people in the world pay 10% or more of their money. Some of the past and present people are: John D. Rockefeller, Henry Ford, Glenn Beck, Bill Gates (both his company and privately), Billionaire David Green, Jon Huntsman, and many more. Mark Victor Hansen repeatedly has said that his book series *Chicken Soup for the Soul* has done as well as it has, because every book donates at least 10% to charitable causes. If some of the richest people in history pay tithing, I suggest you pattern them by paying your tithing. Do they give because they are rich or are they rich because they give? Think about this, are they rich first or are they willing to give first? I suggest they are rich because they give and follow good principles."

"There are two passages I want to share with you to illustrate this concept," Professor Christensen said, and then he pulled out his Bible and read:

> Bring ye all the tithes into the storehouse... and prove me now herewith, saith the Lord of hosts, if I will not open you the windows of heaven, and pour you out a blessing, that there shall not be room enough to receive it.[16]

In another passage, Hezekiah commanded his people, who were starving due to a siege, to pay their tithing—giving what they had.

> And as soon as the commandment came abroad, [the people] brought in... the tithe of all things brought they in abundantly....

> In the third month... when Hezekiah and the princes came and saw the heaps, they blessed the Lord, and his people... [The chief priest replied] Since the people began to bring the offerings into the house of the Lord, we have had enough to eat, and have left plenty: for the Lord hath blessed his people; and that which is left is this great store.[17]

"I want you to notice," said the professor, "these two cited accounts of tithing. In one, we are told that blessings will come greater than we can receive, and in the other, the people not only survive, but thrive. I realize you are students and may not have much money; I come to you as an old farmer. Plant your money seeds by paying your tithing first and finding five hours where you can serve others during the month. Give first to get."

"*As a word of caution, many people say that if they pay their tithing, they will be supported in all their efforts or that they can demand a specific prosperity; **this is not true**. The passages on tithing only sug-*gest opening the windows of heaven—or, giving you the wisdom to act and the ability to receive good things. We still need to adhere to good principles to claim the blessings. Tithing is a catalyst when combined with sound principles."

---

16 Malachi 3:10-12, KJV

17 2 Chronicles 31:5-10, KJV, formatting changed.

"If any farmer stops obeying correct principles—such as taking care of and watering his crops, and willfully neglects his responsibility, then even if he pays his tithing, it's likely that his crops will wither and die. This doesn't mean that tithing failed. It means that the farmer was not following correct principles."

"Wait! Are you going to make us pay 10% of our money just to fulfill an assignment?" Malcolm asked with an obvious tone of panic and annoyance.

"I actually thought about it, because I know the benefit of tithing and service," Professor Christensen said with a smile. "However, I believe that for tithing to work you need to choose to do it for yourself. Service is a different matter. I'm going to require five hours per month. You need to decide if you want to give your tithing by donating 10% of your income to your church, synagogue, mosque, temple, or a cause that you believe in."

"Enough with the preaching," Malcolm blurted out. "Just tell us how to make money."

Another guy responded more favorably and asked in a positive tone, "Does tithing really work? I mean, if I pay 10% of my money, will prosperity really happen?"

"You still have to adhere to correct principles," Professor Christensen replied, ignoring Malcolm's comment, "and if you do so, and pay your tithing, you will prosper in ways you don't know right now. Tithing is a catalyst for good things; you don't get to pick what those good things are, or how they come, but they do come. Does anyone have any examples of paying tithing?" Professor Christensen asked.

Allison quickly responded. "I was once wondering if I should pay tithing when I didn't have a job, but I did it anyway, and the next week I was offered a job."

Justin realized that he had consistently paid his tithing, and he had never starved, but how had tithing helped him? Then he remembered Paul's help with textbooks and all that Paul had taught him, which had saved him some money. Also, he had gotten into this class. "I have always paid my tithing, and my friend showed me how to save money on my school books, and I was given a scholarship—almost by accident.

When I think about these events, I really didn't do too much; they just came to me."

"So you were blessed in ways that you didn't expect but which helped you to prosper with what you needed. Is that right?" asked Professor Christensen.

"Yeah," said Justin, becoming more aware of some of the ways he had been blessed on his trip to Syracuse.

"I know that the critic would say, 'Oh, those things came because of the people you knew or what you did. Those events don't really have anything to do with tithing.' However, God and the universe say, 'Prove me now herewith.' Put it to the test for six months, I say, and you will see a major difference in your life," Professor Christensen said.

"*Now* can we learn about the money stuff?" Malcolm insistently asked.

Professor Christensen replied: "Well, that was some of the most important 'money stuff.' However, for other principles, we'll have to wait till next time. Class is dismissed. Please submit the homework that I will send out in an email."

Chapter 5: Principles and Suggestions

1. Focus on doing things slightly differently that will bring you wealth. Building wealth often doesn't require massive changes, just slight changes.

2. Keeping up with the Jones' is a dangerous game. Spend money on what is truly important to you; avoid the rest. Stay in the rat race only for a time to learn to get out.

3. Tithing is like planting seeds. To grow your money, you need to plant seeds by giving your tithing. Just like real seeds, you get more in return—if you follow correct principles.

4. Be willing to give service to those around you. Giving of yourself allows you to build relationships and often if you teach another, you gain more understanding yourself.

Chapter 5: Warnings and Avoidance

1. Don't assume that if you fail to manage your resources you can expect to maintain the status quo.

2. Tithing is a catalyst for good things; never think that you can demand prosperity because you pay tithing.

3. Even if we pay tithing or serve, we must follow correct principles such as living within our means, investing wisely, and saving for what really matters.

Chapter 6: Writing Right

Justin was really glad he'd enrolled in Professor Christensen's class. He had fun bowling, and he was beginning to see the point of many of the lessons that Professor Christensen was teaching—both directly and indirectly. Plus, the professor was very nice after all, and he even handled Malcolm with courtesy.

After Justin had finished work, he came home and found his roommate Nate doing some type of paperwork. Trying to be polite Justin asked, "Whatcha up to?"

Internship, Scholarship, and Timing Ideas

"I am writing some résumés and cover letters for internships I want to go on next semester." Nate said. "I am looking for an internship that will last through the winter."

"Wait, I thought that internships were in the summer," Justin said confused.

"That's what most people do," Nate responded. "But that is part of the problem: most people take internships in the summer, so there are fewer available. I've found that many companies are willing to hire interns in the fall and winter months—in fact it is often easier to get an internship in the fall or winter than the summer due to less competition."

"That's good to know."

"Yeah, but as an added bonus, I take classes in the summer—the teachers tend to eliminate a lot of the 'busy work' that you can sometimes get—either the semesters are shorter or the teachers don't want to spend the time to put the students through the same quantity of assignments, knowing that they'll need to grade the extra homework in 'their summer break,'" Nate added with a smile.

"Interesting idea," Justin said. "I am going to have to remember that. Just curious, what do you do to help you get noticed as an applicant?"

"Well, I took a class that talked about how to apply to jobs," Nate said, "they taught me a good formula to use."

"What's the formula?" Justin asked.

"Problem + Solution = Results told as a story," Nate said.

"What do you mean by that?" Justin asked.

"Organizations love numbers that can be quantified. Let's say that the pastor asks 10 people to help clean up and weed the church yard. The job takes 2 hours."

Instead of just saying: "I helped clean my church," say something like: "I volunteered as part of a 10-person committee to help make improvements at a local community center to remove debris and improve the landscaping. Our group totaled over 20 hours of improvements, filled 2 dumpsters of discarded materials, and significantly improved the aesthetic appeal of the community center to over 500 active community members who use the community center."

"Can you see a difference?" Nate asked.

"Yeah, with the first, I really don't know what you did. With the second, I was able to get a really good idea of what you did, while making it seem... well, *important*. Why did you call the church a community center?" Justin asked.

"We live in strange times; people have biases against any mention of God, church, and even family. While I don't agree with the notion, and there are many improvements in public acceptance of speaking about God, I try to make it something that other people can relate to. I don't need to tell the review board (unless they ask) that the committee was really five members of my family, or that the community center was a church, but I told the problem, gave solutions, and gave numbers that were measurable—all told as a story. I can do the same thing with school projects, Scouting endeavors, and leadership skills—just don't take it too far, you can over-embellish the story and you will discredit yourself."

"Wait," Justin said, "I don't want to write that every time I try to apply to a job."

"Save your work." Nate said. "You can write it once, put it in a file on your computer, and then copy it later. It becomes a matter of which story do I want to use for any given event. Oh, and one more thing…"

"Yeah, what's that?" Justin asked.

"Something that really helps is if you find out the name of the person or the committee title that'll be reviewing your application. So unless the application requires 'To Whom It May Concern,' don't put it; it is really impersonal and makes the reader feel like he or she is reading a form letter. Say something like 'Dear Members of the A.P.T. Company Review Board' or 'Dear Mr. Jones.' It is so much nicer than a form letter, and shows that you at least have done some research about the organization that you are applying to."

Justin thanked his roommate and left. After the conversation, Justin made a mental note: *I can do that with my scholarships. If I just make a list of stories of my life experiences, and save them, I can speed up how long it will take me to apply to the scholarships. That was really good to hear about the names as well, if I spend less time writing a scholarship essay, I can spend a little more time researching who will actually see my scholarships.* Justin checked his email.

(You can go to *www.CollegeCashChampion.com* and get an Excel Workbook to help you with this.)

Visit Your Dean

True to his word, Professor Christensen sent out an email. The email read:

Dear Class,

Thank you so much for coming bowling with me. I really enjoyed getting to know each of you.

This email does not contain a required assignment—rather, an optional one. I will not follow up with you, but it will help as you apply to scholarships. The assignment is as follows:

Go schedule an interview with the dean, or president, of your major's department; this can be done with the department secretary. Dress up and be on time. Ask him or her: 'Why did you choose the field?', 'What did you enjoy about the field and why specifically did you choose this school?', 'What did you do to help yourself get where you are?', 'What has your career path been like?', 'What are some resources to help students succeed in the department?', and finally, ask your dean if he or she has any questions for you.

The point is NOT to brown-nose, but to introduce yourself and get to know the person who can help you learn a little bit about your major and has the ability to give out scholarships. If you are better known, you have a better chance of being considered. You may want to practice some answers to questions like 'What do you plan to become in your field?', 'When are some times that you have shown leadership?', 'Who is your *sincere* role model and why?', 'When are some times that you have struggled, and been victorious?', and 'What are you doing now to prepare for success?'

The answer to this last question is to tell them about your plan to serve (the 5 hours per month), any study groups or clubs you are part of, and how you are applying to scholarships to help pay for school.

You may want to repeat this exercise with the chair for scholarships (if different than the dean—check with the department secretary). One girl that I know of was majoring in administration. She, instead of interviewing the president of her major, interviewed the president of a university to fulfill a similar assignment while in high school. She said, 'I interviewed him for 15 minutes; he interviewed me for 45 minutes. I now was given a 4-year, full tuition scholarship at this university.'[18] I will second that account, as when I was in college I had similar results with the chair of scholarships for my major. I received a 3-year, full tuition scholarship from my department.[19] Be available for questions about yourself. At the first

18 True account heard by the author in high school.

19 True account done by the author in college.

meeting, the appointment should be about the dean and not yourself, unless asked. You can then set a follow-up visit with the dean in about a month to ask about scholarships.

Now for the Required Assignment:

Go do two activities that are *fun*. You must tell how you found free activities. You must invite a group of at least three people. Excluded activities include TV, movies, and video games. Be creative and have fun, but find ways that you can have fun for free.

Have a great weekend!

–Professor Christensen

Justin was surprised! That was Professor Christensen's homework: Go have fun. He liked his class more.

Justin went to the designated spot on campus, just south of the library, and saw Allison, Ashley, and Tyler. Ashley had invited him along, too. That was okay with Justin, although he was a little disappointed to lose his two-to-one ratio with the girls.

You Benefit by Helping Others

They went into the library. The others were surprised when Justin told them about the homework assignment; none of them had read it yet. Tyler insisted on checking his email to make sure Justin wasn't just trying to have a good time at his expense. When he saw it was the truth, they started discussing some of their ideas.

Ashley spoke first: "Hey, do you remember when we went bowling and Professor Christensen mentioned that millionaires don't focus on activities that don't have a payout? Maybe this is really more of a test to see what we learned and if we will follow principles. Well, I suggest that we go find someone to serve for one of the activities. At least that way we can fulfill some of our service requirement—you know, 'kill two birds with one stone.'"

They all thought that was a great idea. Ideas flowed back and forth about who they could serve, especially on a Saturday. The first idea was tutoring someone, but they didn't know whom to tutor on such short notice.

Then Tyler suggested that they pick up some trash on campus. But when they looked around, they decided the campus actually looked fairly clean. So *that* didn't work.

Allison suggested, "There's a rest home a couple of blocks away from the campus. Why don't we go over there?" They stopped at the rest home. After checking in, they said that they wanted to visit the residents. The attendant said it would be great. So they went from room to room, visiting the residents and asking them how they were doing. The residents' eyes lit up as they saw that somebody was there to see them.

The four students were able to meet a whole lot of different people, and they were even asked to come again. As they were going down the hall, one of the attendants said, "Visiting hours will be ending in about 10 minutes. We need to be able to give the residents lunch."

So, Justin and the others decided that they would say their final good-byes. They went in one last room and saw a sweet old lady. She said that her name was Betty. She was sad, but the girls warmed up very quickly to her. They asked her how she was doing and how she was feeling, and Betty replied that she was doing all right.

Then an attendant came in and said, "Hi, Betty. How's it going today?"

"Well, much better now that these young people are here," Betty replied with a smile.

"Oh, I'm so glad to see that you're visiting her today," the attendant said to the students.

With notice that their time was up, the four headed for the door in a chorus of goodbyes to Betty.

Justin went home and thought about his activities. Professor Christensen had given them the charge to have fun, and Justin thought that this had been a great activity. Plus, it was an excuse to see Allison.

Justin then remembered that he needed to have two activities. He decided to invite his roommates and some of his neighbors to come play a board game. He finished about an hour later.

Justin finished submitting his weekly scholarships from College Board and Fastweb. He copied his submissions and put the submissions onto the class web site.

Essay Ideas

Monday at class, Professor Christensen asked the class to come with him on a field trip. He took them to the campus library where they went into a classroom with computers that Professor Christensen had reserved for his class, with enough computers for everyone.

"Okay," Professor Christensen said, "what were some of your activities you did for free with your groups of three or more?" Class members stated their ideas.

"Played touch football."

"Had a potluck dinner."

"We went to a retirement home."

"Went to a free music concert on campus."

"My friends and I played a board game with others."

"I hope you enjoyed having fun for free," Professor Christensen said. "In today's class we are going to discuss some tips for essays." There were several students who bemoaned the idea till Professor Christensen reminded them about being positive.

"Let's use everyday experiences to describe your abilities to be leaders. What you didn't realize was that by gathering a group together to have fun, you were actually being a leader. People often think that they must have huge and monumental type of leadership positions to be a leader; this is inaccurate. Just because someone may be put near the top of an organization does not automatically make him (or her) the leader—that is just a figurehead, such as a family company where the son inherits the father's business. The son may inherit the title, but may lack the ability to lead the business. Being a leader means that you provide vision and direction and influence by example, not coerce, others to follow you. There are two things that scholarship essays love to see: one is leadership, and the other is service. We are going to discuss some of the ways to present these as essays now."

Professor Christensen turned and wrote on the marker board: "Statement + Problem + Solution = Results as a Story."

Justin remembered part of this equation from his roommate Nate. Justin wondered if there was a correlation.

"Let's take the information," Professor Christensen said, interrupting Justin's thoughts, "from your activities and write two short essays. Let's take, for example, the football game. That means that you had about 10 people, for a small group, or 22 for full size game. What were some of the details?" Professor Christensen asked the student who said 'played touch football.'

"I invited 13 people and 11 of them showed up. We played Saturday morning for about an hour and a half."

"Good," Professor Christensen said, "now let's write an essay. I don't know all the details, but I will make something up; fair enough?"

The student nodded. Professor Christensen continued: "You could write a simple statement saying "'I played football with my friends.' But really that doesn't tell much. Instead, let's use the formula. Statement: 'I have always been a leader.' Let's then use the rest of the formula: 'For example, I invited 13 people in my community to come join me for a morning of physical activity participating in flag football.' This is the statement of the problem, now let's do the solution. 'Eleven of the 13 people invited attended. I coordinated the location, time, and invited the people; also I presented an idea to divide teams. Everyone agreed, and we divided into teams according to my plan. I suggested for my team that someone else be the quarterback because he had a better throwing arm. We played a 10-point game that lasted 1.5 hours. One of the plays was my idea, which led to a touchdown.'"

"Aren't you telling the result, I mean the 1.5 hours and the quantity of people that came, instead of the solution?" the student asked.

"Partially correct," Professor Christensen replied. "Part of the result is mixed in the solution, but let me finish."

"Okay," he said.

"The results are both soft and hard results. For example: 'After playing, several people came up and thanked me for inviting them and said that they would like to play again if I ever arranged another game. Since that game, I invited groups of people and we meet once a week. From this experience I learned true leadership comes as a state of mind: a willingness to involve others, and provide direction with a common goal.'"

"So the results are the measurements, and the lessons learned?"

"You guessed it," Professor Christensen said. "Notice the statement at the beginning and the conclusion at the end; also notice the story: 'I invited people to play football, some showed up, I helped divide the teams, I suggested someone other than me be the star (quarterback) to best use resources, and people enjoyed playing football as a group because of my ability to plan and get people involved.'"

"Got it. Uhh, could you write that down so that I can use it?"

Professor Christensen laughed. "I wouldn't deprive you of the experience—plus, it'll be better if you tell the story."

Overarching Story on an Application

"While we are talking about stories," Professor Christensen continued, "let me tell you about the overall story that you must tell with your scholarship application. There are, generally speaking, three kinds of scholarships: background-based scholarships, project-based scholarships, and merit-based scholarships. Every scholarship can be described as one, or a combination, of these three types."

1) Background-based scholarships are for your heritage, ethnicity, or what progenitors have done. It may be that you come from a certain part of the country, went to a certain high school, have ancestors in a specific ethnic category, or that someone semi-famous was a business partner or pioneer in an industry and left a scholarship legacy. These scholarships are based on your background and exclude individuals that don't fit the mold; you mostly need to be born into, have a parent or step-parent, or be connected to someone who was a forerunner who did something to allow you to get this kind of a scholarship.

2) Project-based scholarships are based more on what you did. Projects consist of writing essays, making a video, doing art work, performing service, etc. This is where your scholarship is based on your effort, or a group effort, to complete something of value. This is like a 'show-and-tell' for scholarships.

3) Merit-based scholarships are determined by an accumulation of things that you have done. Things like a high GPA,

a musical competition, saving someone's life, or discovering a new process or product that benefits others. You have done a series of things to merit the award. Most people cannot show up at a piano recital and expect to win; it takes years of practice to merit the right to play a difficult piece of music extremely well. You must show that your life reflects the scholarship values and guidelines—that you deserve the scholarship.

"No matter what type of scholarship you apply for," Professor Christensen commented, "you should allow your application to tell an overarching story. If you grew up in Maine and someone from your community offered a scholarship for descendants of lobster catchers, and your great-grandfather caught and sold lobsters—even for two years, then your essay needs to reflect that you have heard several of your great-grandfather's stories or how you saw lobster catchers weekly during the summer. Paint a picture for the reader of your application—telling your overarching story, focusing on the type of scholarship, as you are copying and pasting your saved micro-essays."

"What are micro-essays?" Ashley asked.

"Great question. I was about to explain."

"Okay, sorry. I was just curious."

Addressing the rest of the class, the professor continued: "What I want you to do is create micro-essays that are 1-3 paragraphs in length that show attributes of leadership, service, integrity, courage, overcoming hardships, and similar attributes. Write these micro-essays in a word processing program to check grammar and spelling, and then save the micro-essays in Excel or another spreadsheet program, with one essay in each cell. You may want to categorize these by topic such as leadership and service. When you are writing an essay, use these examples from your own life that you previously wrote and saved as micro-essays. You can then copy and paste these segments into your essay to help you to write your paper faster."

Faster Source Citing for Essays

"Big deal," Malcolm exclaimed, "even if I were to copy and paste, that still wouldn't speed me up that much."

"What do you mean? Have you ever tried using micro-essays?" Professor Christensen asked.

"Well, no. I can see your point, and it may speed me up some, but what I meant was I can write fast enough, but I find myself spending more time trying to figure out how to cite my sources. One teacher wants it done in MLA, a scholarship wants it done in Chicago style, another organization wants it in APA; I spend hours just trying to meet their stupid requirements," Malcolm responded with noted sarcasm.

"Interesting problem, what could you do to solve your predicament?"

"I don't know… search the internet to find a grammar book?"

"Class, what is something Malcolm and anyone else could do to help him or her cite sources faster?"

There were several blank stares, but Tyler asked, "Why not use a citation generator?"

"What's that?" several people wanted to know.

"Well," Tyler began, "I needed to find out how to cite some sources for a paper and I did an internet search for 'MLA APA Citation source' and I found something called a citation generator. There were several to choose from and so I played around with a few of them. I could pick the style and then enter a website, ISBN, or title and the generator filled in the rest. Now I don't have to worry about my format as the website does it for free."

"Would you recommend any particular one we can try out now?" Professor Christensen asked.

"Sure. I like *www.citefast.com* because it allows me to instantly create a bibliography in addition to the citations. I just punch in some basic information and it does the rest."

Professor Christensen brought it up in a browser shown on the classroom projector. To try it out, he put in *Success Through a Positive Mental Attitude* and the site asked to confirm which book.

"That's pretty handy," Professor Christensen said, "but I have an idea that could make this work better."

"What's that?" Tyler asked curiously.

"Go to half.com or Amazon.com and enter your book title. This will allow you to use the ISBN and get the right edition, and then copy the ISBN into the Citefast generator. Let's try it." Professor Christensen went to half.com, entered the title, and chose one of the versions. Sure enough, in a matter of a few seconds, there was a perfectly cited source. He did it again, entering a page number. The citation came up perfectly.

"That is really useful, and will go perfectly with the assignment." Then addressing Malcolm, Professor Christensen said in a kind tone, "Did that help you to solve your problem?"

"I guess so."

"I just wanted to show you that simply complaining about a problem rarely solves it. Asking for solutions greatly enhances your capacity to accomplish your goals," Professor Christensen said, to which Malcolm gave a scowl. "Class, I want you to use the remainder of the time to work on your micro-essays."

Justin, who was sitting next to Allison, wrote his two stories about visiting the nursing home and playing games with friends. He and Allison traded friendly jokes about how they would present their visit to the retirement center. He saved his essays in Excel. As Justin finished saving his second essay and was submitting it to the class website, Professor Christensen dismissed the class.

Later that day, while at work, Justin checked his email and found that the campus tuition office had sent him an email.

Dear Mr. Murray,

You have overpaid your tuition. You need to tell us how you would like our office to process the excess of funds.

Sincerely,

Syracuse State University Tuition Office

Justin smiled. *I was able to keep the Pell Grant.* Justin replied indicating that he'd like to have a check made available to him.

After submitting the reply to the tuition office, Justin took the lessons learned from his roommate and Professor Christensen and made some essays about his life experiences, and saved the files in MS Excel and put the file in his email to back it up for future reference. Justin realized: *I just created the beginnings of a system.* (Go to *www.College-eCashChampion.com* to see the videos on essays for more tips.)

Tithing Pains and Blessings

On Sunday, Justin went to church. He gave his tithing on the scholarships, on the FAFSA, and on the money he'd earned at his job. He was amazed. It was largest amount of tithing he ever donated at any one time in his life. He was literally giving hundreds of dollars. The thought did cross his mind about not paying his tithing—after all, he was the one who had done the work.

As he thought about the amount, he remembered Professor Christensen's lesson: by paying it forward was like planting money seeds. He thought about it. He realized that he had been given *thousands* and that he was only asked to give *hundreds*. He gladly put the money into the envelope and went on his way.

As Justin gave his tithing, he remembered that his friend Paul had helped him save money on books; that as he went to buy a book and he just happened to be in the right place at the right time to get his job; he had been awarded a Pell Grant; received several scholarships; and he was enrolled in Professor Christensen's class which was teaching him how to manage his money and learn more about real estate, finance, and business concepts. Justin realized that he had been very blessed—especially when his family was unable to support him. Justin had always paid his tithing, but was only now seeing possibilities of how he had been blessed. Justin decided right then and there, that he would never short change his tithing—it would cost him too much not to pay it.

Chapter 6: Principles and Suggestions

1. Go to see your department's dean.

    a. Make the interview about your dean; find questions that make you sincerely curious about the dean.

    b. This will make you remembered; when your application comes in you will be more likely to be considered.

2. Decide now to apply to many different scholarships and grants during a semester. I recommend 20 to 50 applications.

    a. Go to *www.CollegeCashChampion.com* and see the videos on 'scholarship sequencing', 'fast ways to cite sources,' 'Why Scholarships?'

    b. Use micro-essays and *www.citefast.com* to speed up the time.

3. Scholarships stack. The more you are awarded, the more money goes in your pocket.

4. Find ways to show leadership and positive attributes in everyday activities.

    a. "Statement + Problem + Solution = Results as a Story."

    b. Save your essays into micro-essays, which you can copy and paste.

    c. It works best if you can do this over time.

    d. Find everyday examples of attributes and use these.

5. Save all your essays for school assignments. I recommend backing up your files in your email. With this idea you can:

    a. Ask the teacher/TAs to review your paper and make it better.

    b. Get paid to write your essays by using them for scholarships.

    c. Save time for future essays.

Chapter 6: Warnings and Avoidance

1. If you choose to set an appointment with the dean, DON'T brown-nose.

2. Jack Canfield, *Maximum Confidence*, talks about a young man whose goal was to break every car antenna on the way home. Make your goal realistic, measurable, memorable, beneficial to yourself and others, and fun.

3. Don't just literally copy and paste your essays. Take the time to review each essay and edit it as needed.

Chapter 7: Deciding What You Want

On Tuesday at work, Justin worked on homework, but what he was most excited to do was get some more free money. After having gone to the bank to deposit his paycheck and the check from the surplus of funds from using the Pell Grant and some scholarships, Justin now had thousands of dollars in his account. While he had to wait in line for about 10 minutes, he was so excited to cash his checks. Seeing first-hand that scholarships really are free money, he wanted some more.

Justin knew that he had at this point applied for seven scholarships and had only won two. While he hadn't won five of the scholarships, he had ample proof that they worked. Justin had spent about 24 hours on the seven applications and essays, and had gotten thousands of dollars. Taking the total money he had received from the Pell Grant, the Osborn scholarship, and the $120 he had from his dad's work, he was getting paid hundreds of dollars per hour. *I can't think of a higher paying job; even if I had only gotten the Pell Grant, it would have been worth it.*

What most excited him was that now, thanks to the advice from his roommate and teacher, he had a system. He had his essays ready to go and his information in an Excel sheet. Justin spent the rest of his time at work applying to scholarships from Fastweb. He wanted to refine his system and see how it worked, and so he chose to try it out on scholarships under $1,000 each—saving the more lucrative scholarships for the most time and revisions. He was able to apply to two of these "smaller" scholarships before leaving work with this new system. *It used to take me 3-4 days to do this, but now I can do it in a few hours.*

On Wednesday, Allison and Justin, who were oh-so incidentally sitting in adjacent seats, smiled at each other. Professor Christensen began in an engaging voice, "At the start of class, I introduced the idea of buying a house in college. That is a big goal, but completely possible. We will discuss this in depth later on in the semester. To even begin doing something that big, you must first learn to master your money."

Getting What You Really Want

Justin rolled his eyes a little bit and thought: *Here it comes. He's going to tell us to scrimp and save some more.*

"At the end of this assignment, I'm going to ask you to pick a really big goal to spend your money on, and we're going to create a plan to get there," the Professor said.

Huh? Thought Justin. *Why is he telling us to spend money? Don't all finance guys tell you to scrimp?*

"In fact," Professor Christensen said, interrupting Justin's thoughts, "I want to ask everyone here: 'What's something really fun that you would like to do?' Things like going on a cruise, buying a new electronic gizmo, going on a road trip, getting a ski pass, having a fantastic wedding... what do you *really* want to do, assuming that it was possible? Shout out your answers," the Professor Christensen encouraged.

"I want to go on a road trip to San Diego."

"Go to Six Flags."

"I want to buy a new laptop."

"I want to go on a study-abroad to Europe."

"I'd like to buy a new outfit."

"I want to buy a new tablet."

"I want to buy a bullet bike."

Justin thought for a moment and found himself asking, *What do I really want to do?* He thought about it and then spoke up. "I want to go to Machu Picchu." He had wanted to go since he was in Ecuador, but saying it aloud in front of others made him feel weird.

A few other replies came, including a wedding, flight instruction to get a pilot's license, and a backpacking trip.

"Good," said Professor Christensen. "May I add to the verbal list 'my own property that my roommates pay off' and 'a successful business'?" he asked. "I want to help you all obtain your dreams. Let me share two quotes with you and then tell you a story. Will Rogers said, 'Too many people spend money they haven't earned, to buy things they don't want, to impress people they don't like.'"[20]

"I'd be willing to guess that everyone here could, in less than one hour and with the aid of the Internet, spend a million dollars, if it were given to them, and if they had the desire to spend it. College makes it incredibly easy to spend money on useless junk that doesn't matter. There is *never* an income high enough that you can't outspend it. As a Japanese proverb says: 'Getting money is like digging with a needle, spending it is like water soaking into sand.'[21] It is so easy to spend money on worthless junk; I am asking you to spend your money on what matters to you and give up the insignificant things."

Never an Income Big Enough You Can't Outspend

"My parents-in-law, my mother- and father-in-law, went to college earning a student wage, which, if you stop and think about it, isn't much at all. They did just fine living on that small amount, having a food budget of $5 per week! They never went into debt. Well, my father-in-law got employed after graduation and suddenly started making five times their combined previous student wages, and they were blown away. My parents-in-law were like, 'Wow! How are we ever going to spend this much?' But it didn't take long. All of a sudden, they started asking themselves by the end of the month, 'Where did our money go?' They decided to write down every purchase they make to find out where they were spending their money. To their great surprise, they found that their money was disappearing due to a bunch of little nickel-and-dime types of things that they were buying—50 cents here, two dollars there, 25 cents there."

"Obviously, 50 cents back then was worth more than it is now, but the point is that my parents-in-law stopped being aware of their spend-

---

20 Goodreads. "Quote by Will Rogers: "Too many people spend money they haven't earned...."Accessed April 19, 2014. www.goodreads.com/quotes/42553-too-many-people-spend-money-they-haven-t-earned-to-buy.

21 Quoteland.com. "Money Quotes." Accessed April 19, 2014. www.quoteland.com/topic/Money-Quotes/101/.

ing. The money disappeared because they didn't control their spending habits. They were not spending *'on purpose.'* Fortunately, my father-in-law made corrections that we'll talk about in a moment.[22] Now I am NOT going to tell you to write down every penny, but I will show you a system so that you won't need to worry about your money."

"If you are spending your money on useless items, it's time to become *aware* of how you're spending your money. You don't have to eliminate *all* useless spending, just most of it. What do I mean by useless items and useless spending? A small bag of chips that costs $4 at a snack shop; eating fast food every day; letting food go to waste; going to new releases on multiple movies per year; new gaming consoles or games, and so on. Spending your money on things that you don't truly value, or that offer fleeting satisfaction, is called your *Bubblegum-Diamond Thief.*

"What's that?" A girl asked.

"A *Bubblegum-Diamond-Thief* is what costs you money. To illustrate, let me ask you: how long does bubblegum last?

"Maybe two hours," she said with a shrug.

"How long would your mother keep her wedding ring diamond?"

"Forever; she'd never let it go."

"Why the difference in time for those two items?"

"The diamond has value and reminds her of how much she loves my dad, while the bubblegum is worthless after it has been used."

"That is exactly the point. If you buy too many bubblegum type of items, or items that only offer temporary satisfaction, you lose out on your diamond type items, or the items that you really want and really matter to you."

Bubblegum-Diamond-Thieves—Avoid Debt

"Let me give you an analogy. Has anyone here ever used a coupon?" Several class members nodded. "Can you ever imagine going to the checkout register and handing the clerk a coupon that said 'pay an additional 15%?' The clerk gives you a 15% discount, but you correct

---

22 This is a true story of the author's real father- and mother-in-law.

the clerk and say 'No, no, no, this coupon was to cost me 15% more—so 115% of the purchase price. Please change my order; I wanted to pay 15% more.' Can you imagine the confused look on the clerk's face?"

"Why would anyone actually do that?" Justin asked.

Professor Christensen smiled. "I agree!" He said with emphasis, "Why *would* anyone hand the clerk a coupon to pay more? But people do it every day when they pay with credit cards and don't pay them off—only instead of 15% they pay up to 29%, and then carry a balance from year to year. Instead of buying something else, people waste money paying interest."

Justin got the point: *Interest is an expensive waste of cash.*

"What are some other ways college students waste money?" Professor Christensen asked the class.

"Alcohol and cigarettes."

"Fast food."

"Gasoline."

"Clothes and makeup," a guy said.

"*Videogames and cars,*" a girl retorted.

"Okay," interjected Professor Christensen. "Let's keep it friendly, but you can easily see the point: money can disappear in an instant, but take a long time to regain. I'm glad you listed cars. Having a car, even if it is fully paid off, costs about $300 per month to own. The average monthly costs are: $100 for gasoline, $100 for insurance, and $100 as an averaged-per-month-cost for licensing, maintenance, repairs, and registration. $300 is a lot of money when you only make $1,000 to $2,000 per month—before taxes. You may get a car to get a higher paying job that is farther from campus. However, after subtracting the approximate $300 extra cost, you have to ask yourself if the job is actually paying you more. If you can get a job for $8 per hour on campus and a job that pays $10 per hour 20 minutes from campus, you should pick the $8 per hour job as it will save you time and money. Cars are *Bubblegum-Diamond-Thieves* that are really sneaky because you feel as if it is a justifiable expense that actually costs you money. You need to ask yourself: 'Am I willing to spend $300 a month or more to own a car?' If not, sell it and buy a bicycle or student bus pass."

"I want teach you both proactive strategies to earn money, and defensive strategies to keep money. You need both to win the money game. (You can go to *www.CollegeCashChampion.com* and watch two videos on *'The Bubblegum-Diamond-Thief'* and *'The Awesome Factor.'*")

Spending on Purpose

"This is why I recommend that you pick something fun, something that you really want. You have the ability to *choose* how you spend your money. Get your friends involved in this. Plan a really big event, such as going to Europe, going on a road trip, or something else you want, and get your friends involved. Tell them, 'In 13 months, let's go do _____(whatever your goal is) together. And let's start saving now.' You'll find that people are usually 'on board' to do something fun or adventurous, and planning in advance adds to the adventure and possibilities."

"This also becomes your beacon at the moment of decision. You can decide how to spend your money. When you're shopping or when friends want to go out and splurge, remind yourself that you're saving up to do your fun activity—or your *Diamond*. Tell your friends something like, 'I'm saving up for a road trip (or whatever). How about we *rent* a movie, instead of going to the theater?' Simply purchasing your food from the store—and saving dining out for important planned events—really helps to save money. So, class, I want to teach you how to spend your money the *smart* way, on purpose."

Offense + Defense + Strategy = Success

"Class, throughout this class I am going to share with you fast ways to make and keep money. You will need to have offensive and defensive strategies."

"Do I have anyone here that likes sports?" Several people nodded or raised their hands. "Can anyone tell me which sport you will win if you strictly use defense?" No answer came.

"Alright, how about if your strategy is strictly offense—would you win?"

"If you can score more points than the other team," a girl ventured.

"Okay," the professor stated, "what sport do you play?"

"Basketball."

"If you were to try to score and the other team was to defend you, it would take your team around 20 seconds per shot to make a basket—if not more. But if you were to not have any players at the opposing basket to defend, the other team would be able to make a shot in probably 10 seconds if they staggered their players. Even if they missed, because your team is playing strictly offense they would be the only team going after the ball, and their team would get the rebound. Just on time, they would be more likely to win because it took them only 10-20 seconds to make a shot, whereas it took you 20-35 seconds to score. The other team would win even if your players were more skilled offensively; the only exception would be if their defense was so bad that it wasn't even a challenge, but even then you would have to score faster than they did to get more points."

"But if I were to use offense and defense, I am still not guaranteed to win," the girl retorted.

"True, but your odds of success go up drastically using both," Professor Christensen replied. "But if you use both principles, it then comes down to strategy and skill, along with consistent effort. Even if your skills were to be *unstoppable*, your strategy could sink your game; on the other hand, if you had a great strategy but no skills, you would lose. You need to strategize using offense and defense and increase your skills. Lastly, if you did nothing to implement or practice both, you would be out of shape."

The girl nodded in agreement.

Assignment for Offense and Defense

Professor Christensen again addressed the class. "Within the past few weeks you were given the assignment to apply to FAFSA and at least four scholarships. As an offensive strategy, I am going to assign that everyone here apply to 20 scholarships. You only need 16 more to fulfill the assignment; whether you want to do them all at once or over the semester, it doesn't matter to me, but they need to be done, and submitted to the class website. This is an offensive strategy. Let's take a vote: would you rather have me give you an offensive or defensive strategy that you can immediately use?"

"If by offense you mean making more money, let's do that one first," Tyler said. "I could use the extra cash."

Other students readily agreed. Professor Christensen smiled and said: "I knew that you would pick that one. It almost always is chosen first. It is a lot more interesting to make money—or at least that is what people think. Before I tell you the strategy, I want you to remember: *It is what you keep—not make, that matters*. Nonetheless, I'll teach you all a proactive money tip."

An Idea to Get Your Employer to Pay for Tuition

"Go to your employer's human resource department and ask if there is a tuition assistance or reimbursement program, and what is required to participate. Get the details and see if you are eligible. Most employers will require that you stay with the company for at least a year; however, if you ever are required to pay all or part back, it usually comes interest free as part of a re-payment plan. This is far better than a student loan because you don't have to pay interest. However, if you get to keep the money, this is a great resource."

"If your employer does not presently offer a tuition reimbursement program, tell your employer this: 'I have found a way to reduce the company's taxes that will save the company from having to pay thousands of dollars.' Your employer, or boss, will be interested at the sound of tax savings. Then say, 'As of August of 2012, one of the tax exemptions allowed by the IRS is that employers can deduct educational expenses up to $5,250, per employee, each year by offering tuition reimbursement. If I were to go to the company accountant and verify this fact of how much the company would save, would you be willing to save money on taxes by helping to pay for my tuition expenses?' Keep in mind that your employer may add other conditions, but just by asking you can save yourself money by getting this. Now one important fact is: whether or not you are getting tuition reimbursement from your employer, be the best employee that you can. You never know at the end of the year, or another point, if your boss will decide to offer this to you. Show you are a good employee and investment."

"But that seems like so much work," Ashley complained. "Besides, I'd be so nervous to talk to my boss."

"Ok," said Professor Christensen, "which requires more work: spending maybe an hour getting the requirements for tuition reimbursement to get $0 to $5,250, working about 600 hours at $10/hour to get the $5,250 after taxes, or spending 10–20 years paying back student loans? Any one of those three methods can help you pay for tuition, but it only would take about 10 minutes to ask and 45 minutes to fill out any paperwork to get the tuition reimbursement, instead of 10 years with student loans."

"Well, if you put it that way." Ashley said, "I guess it would be easier to at least see if I could get tuition reimbursement—but I am still afraid to talk to my boss."

"Class, what could someone who is scared to talk to a boss do to help him or her ask about tuition reimbursement?"

"Practice on a friend."

"Schedule an appointment to talk."

"Bring in your recent positive employee evaluation to add credibility."

"Send an email to HR."

"Email your boss."

"Great ideas," said Professor Christensen. "Let's move on to defensive strategies." (For more ideas on how to do this, please go to *www.CollegeCashChampion.com* and see the videos on 'getting your employer to pay for school.')

Start of Defensive Strategies

"For defense," Professor Christensen continued, "every person should read or listen to David Bach's book or audio book, *Debt Free for Life*. I cannot tell you how ridiculously people behave, including many of our local, state, and federal governments, spending more money than they bring in. And they have to work harder to pay off the interest. I hope that you really take this lesson of getting what you really want and managing your money to heart."

"As an additional strategy, I want you to pick one to three goals that are meaningful to you. You need to make a realistic plan to save up for that goal (i.e. $X per month, take a second job, start a business, eliminate ___ activity that you don't really value—saving you $Y dollars per period, or something similar). We are going to then use these goals next class."

"Whoa," said Malcolm. "All these X's and Y's, you'd think we were in a math class."

Professor Christensen chuckled along with several class members. "Out of fairness, you do get math credits for taking the class, but don't worry—nothing too hard to grasp."

Professor Christensen gave some assignments for real estate that he introduced. The assignments were not hard, but they did require some understanding. Justin wondered if Allison would be willing to form a study group with him; he really didn't need the help, but it was a nice thought of having an excuse to see her and get to know her better.

Scholarships May Stack (Apply to as Many as You Can)

Justin got up and left class. "This is going to be easy and fun," Allison said. "Our assignment is to plan how we're going to have fun and make a plan of how to get there."

"I think I will enjoy this." Justin replied. "I'm starting a study group to help with the other assignments. Would you like to join? We can ask some other classmates as well."

"That sounds great." Allison replied, "Why don't we invite Ashley?" Justin agreed and, after asking Ashley, the three of them exchanged emails and phone numbers. They agreed upon a night to meet up and go over the assignment.

After a few hours, Justin's chat window sounded. '*Pling.*' Justin's dad started chatting with him.

"Hey Justin, how are you?"

"Good," Justin replied, "College has been fun."

"I feel really bad that I could not provide for your college like I said I would. Are you doing all right?"

"Dad, don't worry. I have already paid for tuition, books, and my rent for this month."

"Do you need anything?"

"Dad, I am in a class that is teaching me how to apply for scholarships, manage money, etc. Don't worry, I'll be fine."

Justin was surer of that statement as he thought about what Professor Christensen had taught him, and now that he had more money because of the Pell Grant, he was excited.

"I forgot to tell you and Mom, I was awarded a scholarship for incoming freshmen, plus I was given a Pell Grant—I can keep the extra money. With my job, I'll be fine."

"Well, a fine time to tell your family."

"Sorry, I've been busy."

"Don't worry about it, but we're glad to hear that you are doing well. Keep us posted."

"I will."

Justin and his dad chatted for a little longer. His dad had taken a second job to help make ends meet. Justin was so grateful for Professor Christensen's assignment to apply early for scholarships. It had 'saved his bacon.' He decided that he was going to apply to as many scholarships as he could this semester. Justin logged into Fastweb and started looking for other scholarships.

Chapter 7: Principles and Suggestions

1. Go to see your department's dean.

    a. Make the interview about your dean; find questions that make you sincerely curious about the dean.

    b. This will make you remembered; when your application comes in, you will be more likely to be considered.

2. Decide now to apply to many different scholarships and grants during a semester. I recommend 20 to 50 applications.

    a. Go to *www.CollegeCashChampion.com* and see the videos on 'scholarship sequencing', 'Why Scholarships?'

3. Pick a really big goal and make a viable plan to get what you really want (i.e. $X per month, take a second job, start a business, eliminate ___ activity that you don't really value—saving you $Y dollars per period, or something similar).

    a. Use this goal to help make a plan.

    b. What is something that you really want?

    c. Don't worry too much about the 'How'—just create a simple basic plan and later we can discuss more details.

4. Learn about both offensive and defensive money strategies.

5. Scholarships generally stack. The more you are awarded, the more money goes in your pocket.

Chapter 7: Warnings and Avoidance

1. If you choose to set an appointment with the dean, DON'T brown-nose and dress up for the appointment.

2. Make your goal to benefit you and other people—something that creates a good memory and helps others. Jack Canfield, *Maximum Confidence*, talks about a young man whose goal was to break every car antenna on the way home. Make your goal realistic, measurable, memorable, beneficial to yourself and others, and fun.

3. Don't try to do exclusively offense or defense; both are needed for financial success.

4. Apply early to scholarships. The earlier you can apply, the more likely you will have the money when you need it.

5. Don't assume that the university/college will tell you that you have an excess of funds; you need to check with them.

Chapter 8: Money Mastery

Justin applied for three scholarships over the next two days; two of them were for under $1,000, so the application was not as in depth. With the third, Justin wanted to use an essay he had written for another class; it turned out that he could use parts of the essay, but needed to modify it. Following his roommate Nate's advice, this time when he applied, he made an MS Excel file with the commonly asked questions, like his first name, last name, major, high school GPA, class standing, address, etc. Justin also created some micro-essays. He was able to submit the two smaller scholarships in less than three hours. Justin did screenshots in the class website.

Justin saved his Excel file so that the next time he applied to a scholarship, it was then a matter of copy and paste for the repetitive fields. It was really easy. While Justin had only been awarded a few scholarships at this point, he was still willing to apply so that he would have the option of getting money. *It's like Mr. Wheatley's example about flying standby: If I apply, I might get a scholarship, but if I don't at least apply, I won't.*

Justin's Goals—Finding Your Motivation

Justin wanted to take Professor Christensen's assignment regarding his goals seriously. He submitted the following:

1. Go to Machu Picchu in 18 months for spring break.

2. Graduate without student loans or credit card debt.

3. Buy a property before I graduate.

Justin's first goal was his motivating goal. He was excited because he had wanted to go ever since being in Ecuador; it had become a dream. The other goals were indefinite, as he didn't know the exact timing or how. Justin decided for his basic plan that he was going to save $30 every two weeks from his paychecks. Also, he was going to pay half of whatever unexpected money came his way from things like birthdays and Christmas toward his goals.

You Don't Have to Spend Much to Have Fun

Justin really wanted to take Allison out on a date. He just didn't know how to make the transition. It was one thing to have her as a study-buddy and homework helper, it was a completely different matter to ask her out. Justin figured, "Well, I guess the best thing to do is to just ask her." So, he came up with several ideas—going to a park and playing Frisbee, or going to play tennis (he could offer to teach her if she didn't know how to play), or finding a local hike to go on. Afterwards they could go to dinner.

Justin asked his roommates where a good, but inexpensive place to go eat might be. "Why not invite her here for dinner or go on a picnic together?" one of his roommates suggested. "At least that way, if things go south… you are not shelling out a lot of cash for a first date. I mean, you can always take her out to eat later when your relationship develops."

"That's a really good idea," Justin said. Justin thanked his roommates and started making plans. After deciding on a picnic—Justin didn't know how Allison would feel being invited to his place on the first date; Justin thought that it would be best to eat at the park. Justin planned a menu and realized just how valuable his roommate's advice was: Justin didn't even know if Allison was dating someone else, or if she was even interested in going out with him. At least by doing a picnic, he wasn't out $20-$40 for a first date with Allison.

Justin and Allison had exchanged phone numbers at one study group and he had put it in his phone already. Grabbing the bull by the horns, he gave her a call.

"Hello, Allison. This is Justin from cl—"

"Hi, Justin! How are you?" Allison answered.

"I'm doing alright. Hey, I was wondering if you'd like to go to a park to play tennis or go biking and then have a picnic with me this Saturday."

She said, "Yeah! That sounds great! What did you have in mind?"

"I'd like to go play tennis, but if you don't know how to play, we can go play Frisbee or go biking."

"That sounds fun, let's go play tennis. I once had a roommate who taught me a little."

"That sounds good. I have two rackets and some tennis balls. We can meet up at the park or I can meet you on campus, which do you prefer?"

"We always seem to be on campus. Why don't we head to a park?"

Justin said, "All right. I'll come by and pick you up at three o'clock on Saturday? Will that work?"

"Sounds good to me, but if the park is not too far, could we walk?"

"Yeah, I think that will work."

"Great," Allison said, "I will see you then." They ended the call pleasantly.

Yes! Justin couldn't help thinking, after the call.

Well, Saturday came and Justin was surprised how nervous he was, especially since he had already done so much with her. But this was different: this was a date. Justin arrived at Allison's apartment a little early, did a breath and B.O. check and went to the door. Allison answered.

Justin smiled and was about to comment on her outfit of a T-shirt and basketball shorts, but before he could say anything, she said "Hey, Justin, you look really nice today!"

"Thanks," he said. "I was about to say the same to you."

"Thanks," Allison said with a smile.

"So, are you ready to play?"

"Yeah!"

Justin and Allison walked to the park, and went to the tennis court. "You said that your roommate taught you a little bit of how to play. Would you like any tips on how to play? Or we could just start on a game."

"Why don't we just start on a game?" Allison said.

They started to play and Justin was impressed. Her swing was pretty good! You could tell that she was a novice tennis player, but she did well.

"Hey, you're pretty good."

"Yeah, I used to play softball in high school," Allison said. "I guess it kind of carries over."

"You are full of surprises!"

Justin let Allison win a game, but he won twice. Both had fun. Allison and Justin went to a nearby grassy field and started getting the food out.

"I hope you like Ecuadorian food, 'cuz that's what we're having."

"Smells good."

"They're papusas—kind of a grilled sandwich."

They sat down once they got their food and started talking. Justin found out that Allison's dad was a barber and that she was paying her own way through college.

Justin described his family and some of the events that had happened in his life. Then he talked about his humanitarian service that he had done a few years ago, and she talked about always having wanted to go study abroad. The rest of the evening went fairly well. After their dinner, Justin walked Allison to her apartment and walked home.

Parable of Instant Returns

At class Professor Christensen had everyone sit in a semicircle around him. He then asked, "Who wants to trade 10 dollars to receive 20 dollars?" Everyone raised a hand.

Professor Christensen repeated, "Who wants to trade 10 dollars to receive 20 dollars?" Again, everyone raised his or her hand, or made comments of acceptance.

For a third time, the professor asked, "Who wants to trade 10 dollars to receive 20 dollars?"

Most students raised their hands, but a student named Tyler got up and went to his backpack, pulled out his wallet, and removed a 10-dollar bill. He walked over to Professor Christensen, handed him the 10-dollar bill, and said, "I do." Professor Christensen pulled out a crisp 20-dollar bill and handed it to Tyler. Professor Christensen then asked the class:

"Excluding those who already participated, who wants to trade five dollars to receive 10 dollars?"

The students now understood what game Professor Christensen was playing. This time, students began jumping up for their wallets and purses. It was a race among students, and Allison got there first.

"Here's five dollars," Allison said. Professor Christensen handed her the 10-dollar bill and received the five-dollar bill. Professor Christensen began again:

"Excluding those who've already participated, who wants to trade two dollars to receive five dollars?"

Justin didn't have his wallet, and he didn't have any cash on him, so he watched as five dollars were exchanged for two dollars. When it hit one dollar for two dollars, one student tried to write an I.O.U. note, but Professor Christensen said he only accepted cash.

"Either you have it, or you don't," the professor said.

The student returned to his seat in the semicircle. One dollar was traded for two dollars, and the one-dollar bill went into Professor Christensen's pocket. Students started griping that they didn't have their money.

"Remember our rule about being positive," Professor Christensen said in a cheerful tone. The students got the message and stopped their complaints.

"How did it feel to watch others getting a deal while you didn't, knowing that if you had had the available cash, you would have gladly made the same deal for yourself?" the professor asked the class.

"Jealous."

"Eager."

"Anticipating how I could get cash."

"Upset!"

The students answered nearly all at once.

"I want you all to learn some very big lessons from this example," Professor Christensen said. "First, money talks, words walk. In other words, you can only take advantage of opportunities if you have the cash available—it may not be *your* cash, but you do need to have it available. Second, it *is* possible to make an instant return on your money. Third, I needed to get a dollar for a toll road, and the attendant never has the right change," the professor added with a smile. The students laughed.

"How can we apply these lessons?" Professor Christensen asked.

"Always carry cash," Tyler said.

"Well, I would recommend that you decide on how much is right for you," Professor Christensen replied. "But for students, carrying about 10 dollars on your person may be a good idea... but consider carrying a pre-paid debit or pre-paid credit card which may work as cash. It's more secure than cash, but allows you to keep inside pre-defined limits. What else did you learn from this example?"

Justin raised his hand and said, "It was more than just having the cash; it was also taking action with that cash. When you first asked us about trading the $10 for $20, every one of us raised our hand, but only that one who was willing to get out of his seat and take action received any of the money."

"Good," said the professor. "We're taught to raise our hands, and while that is movement, it is not action that leads you to the goal. Excellent! What else can we learn?"

Allison responded. "We can learn from watching others and then take similar actions."

"What do you mean?" the professor asked Allison.

"Well, when Tyler got up and exchanged his 10 dollars for 20, we all watched. I figured something similar might happen again, so I pulled out my wallet."

"Great!" the professor said. "We can learn both things to *do* and things to *avoid* by watching others. Whom you watch also matters: if you learn from a garbage man, you can learn how to gather garbage; if you learn from a millionaire, you can learn how to be a millionaire. Brian Tracy said, 'Model the best people in your industry. Imitate what the best do.'[23] If we can learn to do what people who manage their money well do, then we can learn from them. Any other lessons learned from the example?"

Ashley raised her hand. "I have a question. You said a moment ago that it's possible to get an instant return on your money. Could you explain how to do that?"

"Glad you asked," the professor responded. "There are *slow* ways to wealth, medium ways, faster ways, plain *dumb luck*, and dishonest methods to earn money. In this class, we're going to address all of them.

"First, the luck and dishonest methods: win the lottery, inherit money, win a sweepstakes, win a tournament, cheat, lie, steal, defraud others, run a scam, and take credit for someone else's work. These methods are mostly determined by chance (specific non-repeatable situations) and poor ambition. While they can happen, they are not repeatable for everyone: just because you know someone who did something dishonest and got away with it, it doesn't mean that you will be as fortunate. Just because you see someone win the lottery, it doesn't mean you'll be able to win. Most of these events happen by chance; they are almost impossible to replicate and are really a waste of time, effort, energy, and money.

"In respect to the lottery, Roger Jones said, 'I think of lotteries as a tax on the mathematically challenged.'[24] Irrespective of who you are, for each lottery ticket that you buy, your chances of picking six correct

23 Tracy, Brian. *Flight Plan How to Achieve More, Faster Than You Ever Dreamed Possible.* San Francisco, Calif: Berrett-Koehler Publishers, 2008.

24 Jones, Roger. "Quotes About Lottery." Good Reads. Accessed April 19, 2014. http://www.goodreads.com/quotes/tag/lottery.

numbers between one and ninety-nine are fewer than one out of eighty billion—even worse if sequence matters. Most of the people who play the lottery are the poorer class of people,[25] as they expect to 'hit it big.'[26] They dream of easy wealth but are unwilling to do what most of you did today; that is, taking action towards the goals. You won't find many millionaires playing the lottery. True, there are some who play, but on the whole, millionaires realize it's a game of chance and a waste of time and money."

"Additionally, for those who win the lottery, their *lives* also change drastically, as winners are often threatened, sued, and sometimes killed.[27] Even if those negative events didn't happen, there is a greater sense of satisfaction in earning the money *yourself*—the 'I built this!' 'I accomplished this!' and 'I overcame this!' attitudes you get from following principles that require you to think, work, and grow. Lotteries, inheritances, tournaments, contests, or other lucky wins deprive you of that satisfaction, and since you didn't earn it, you don't value it as much. My goal is to help you all gain financial independence. Since we cannot replicate with accuracy the *lucky* approach, we are eliminating it from this class, and I suggest eliminating it from your lives because it is a waste of time and money."

Turning to Ashley, the professor said, "After that long-winded explanation of something to *avoid*, let me tell you how to slowly build wealth, and this will more directly answer your question about getting an instant return."

401(k) Plans and Benefits of Starting Early

"This is a slower method, but it's literally the same thing as our example of exchanging money at the beginning of class today. If your employer matches 25%, then for every $10 you put in, you get $12.50, total—your $10 plus $2.50—or up to whatever limit set by your em-

---

25 Clotfelter, Charles T. "Do Lotteries Hurt the Poor? Well, Yes and No." Duke Policy News. Accessed April 19, 2014. http://news2.sanford.duke.edu/newsletters/dpn/summer00/lottery.html.

26 Hopkins, Christopher A. "Personal finance: Lottery mania hurts low-income players." Times Free Press. Accessed April 19, 2014. http://www.timesfreepress.com/news/2012/dec/05/1205c-personal-finance-lottery-mania-hurts-low/.

27 'Hannah'. "How the Lives of 10 Lottery Millionaires went Disastrously Wrong." money.co.uk. Accessed April 19, 2014. http://www.money.co.uk/article/1002156-how-the-lives-of-10-lottery-millionaires-went-disasterously-wrong.htm#ixzz2LlGOA2mb.

ployer. For the one-to-one match, for every $10 you put in, you get another $10. Keep in mind that for any 401(k) plan, your employer will probably request that you stay for at least a year, but if you ever quit or change jobs, you can take all that money with you and put it in your new job's 401(k) plan or you can roll it over to an IRA.

The advantage is that your money is working for you. The stock market has averaged about 10% annual return over a 15-to-20-year period.[28] The earlier you can start a 401(k), the more time your money has to grow. And not only does your money grow, but your employer's *match* also grows.

"Let me show you how much your money can grow in 40 years. If you were to put in $100 each month, and that was matched by your employer with another $60 (a 60% contribution match—60% being a semi-average match rate) for a total of $160 per month, and then just did this until retirement at each job you have for 40 years, averaging a 10 percent return, then you would have over $1.02 million and would have put in a total of $48,000 of your personal money. If you had wanted to reach $1 million in only 10 years instead of 40, then you would have had to put in $279 each month, again matched at a 60% match, to reach over a $1 million—putting in over $100,000 of your own money. It really is the *time* that compounds the interest that you want on your behalf. That is making your money work for you.

"One great thing about 401(k) plans is that they take money out before tax. So $100 pre-tax is like $75 after tax, if you're in a 25 percent income tax bracket. Let's say that you put in the $160 per month where there is a 60 percent match, as mentioned above, for five years—$100 is your contribution before tax. At the end of five years, assuming no employer loss, mathematically the total would be $12,389.90. Then let's say that after graduation you are hired by a company and put $5,000 per year into your 401(k) plan, or $416.67 each month, for another five years, again assuming a 60 percent match by your employer. At the end of the 10 years, you would have $52,650.90. Now let's say that times are hard, and you never again put another cent into the plan after the initial 10 years. Assuming a mathematical 10 percent aver-

---

28 Anspach, Dana. "Historical Stock Market Returns—Stock Market Returns Since 1973." About.com Money Over 55. Accessed April 19, 2014. http://moneyover55.about.com/od/howtoinvest/a/marketreturns.htm

age return for the next 30 years, how much would you have when you retire?"

The students started guessing. "$650,000?" "$300,000?" "$575,000?"

"All good guesses, but all of them are far too low," Professor Christensen said. "Mathematically, you would have $1.04 million before tax and would only have put in a total of $31,000 of your own money."

Many students couldn't believe it.

"Let me explain further," the professor said. "Let's say that you put in the $416.67 per month for 30 years. You would have over $2 million. In contrast, let's say that you didn't start now, but you waited 10 years and then started putting in the $416.67 a month and continued for 20 years with that same amount. How much would you have?"

A student made a guess. "One million dollars."

Someone else suggested, "You'd still have two million, minus the twelve thousand."

Another student piped up: "One point five million."

Professor Christensen corrected the students. "You would have $941,878. You see, you cost yourself over a million dollars at the time of retirement by waiting 10 years. While it may appear it doesn't matter, it's the compounding that you want most. Starting early makes a big difference."

"This is why Albert Einstein stated, 'Compound interest is the eighth wonder of the world. He, who understands it, earns it; he, who doesn't, pays it.[29]'"

Justin raised his hand and said, "Excuse me, Professor. Aren't you predicting that the stocks will always return 10%? I mean, didn't we just have a 2008/2009 meltdown? During those years, it was all over the news that values were lost, and people lost a lot of money. Aren't 401(k) plans tied to stocks?"

Professor Christensen smiled and said, "Yes, they are. To put it simply, if you put $10 in your 401(k), and your employer matched it

---

29 Einstein, Albert. "Compound interest is the eighth wonder of the world" Good Reads. Accessed April 19, 2014. www.goodreads.com/quotes/76863-compound-interest-is-the-eighth-wonder-of-the-world-he.

to equal $10 + $10 = $20, the 401(k) plan manager then takes the $20 and invests it in mutual funds. Mutual funds are a collection of stocks managed by a professional team. A mutual fund generally prevents you from 'keeping all your eggs in one basket.'" If your account were to lose 50% of its value, you would have $10 if you sold during this time. This is why you must average over time."

"When stock prices go down, if you invest the same amount every month, you can buy more shares when the prices are low. When the prices rise, you have added value, provided you didn't sell when the prices were low. This is referred to as *Dollar-Cost Averaging*, where you decide to pay the same amount of money each month and the price averages out over time. People only lost money in the stock market if they sold when the prices were low, or invested in investments that were overpriced and never returned to previous values. Looking forward to this year, the original values returned to previous and new highs. Additionally, the money that was put in during the time of the fall and rise basically averaged out."

"The question always comes up: 'I don't know what to invest in; where do I start?' Companies know this question will arise, so that's why they created what are called *life cycle funds,* also known as *target date funds*. Any reputable, well-known, financial services company can help you find these funds. Check with your plan manager and ask about life cycle funds, or target date funds. They balance your funds automatically in different types of stocks, bonds, money market funds, and treasury notes, with some even allowing you to invest in both foreign and domestic markets."

"When you're younger, you want your money to grow so that it can pay you more money. When you're older, you need to be more conservative, keeping your money from loss so that you can use it. Life cycle funds, or target date funds, automatically adjust your investing strategies, and you select them according to when you plan to retire. Professional money managers do most of your investing for you."

"The key is to set it up automatically. It'll be deducted from your paycheck, and you won't even notice it after a while. Set it up once and it's done. Starting early has a big advantage. You can learn more by going to

http://financialmentor.com/calculator/retirement-calculator and

http://cgi.money.cnn.com/tools/savingscalc/savingscalc.html from
Financial Mentor and CNN Money and using their financial calculator...

"A 401(k) plan takes money out before tax. So $100 pre-tax is like
$75 after tax, if you're in a 25% income tax bracket."

Managing Taxes—Don't Lose Money

"Now let's talk about how to manage taxes," Professor Christensen
continued.

"Let's suppose," the professor said, "that you earn $1,000 per
month—for easy math. The biggest thing for college students to learn
is *cash flow*—where your money flows *from* and where it flows *to*.
Most college students don't make enough to pay income taxes at the
end of the year, so if you simply go to your human resource department
and change your W4 exemptions to be greater, you'll have more of
your money coming to you. Getting a tax refund means that you gave
an interest free loan to the government. Changing your exemptions
will increase your paycheck."

Malcolm piped up, "How to cheat on taxes! This is my kind of
lesson!"

"This is, in fact, very legal," Professor Christensen responded.
"Unfortunately, allocating your W4 exemptions, and contributing to
your 401(k) plan are all part of the game that the present tax code requires that we play."

Justin was beginning to see more clearly the reason to manage taxes and contribute to a 401(k): *prevent unnecessary losses from being
deducted so that he could have more available cash.*

"The last thing with tax management," the professor continued, "is
to learn to use taxes to your benefit. Keep track of your tuition, books,
and housing expenses while in school; you may need them to do your
taxes. In a future class, we will be discussing how to use these records
of schooling costs to your advantage."

Direct Deposit and High Yield Accounts

"Let me briefly change topics by asking a question," Professor Christensen said. "Who here would like to make money on their everyday money?"

"Isn't that like asking: 'Who'd like to eat ice cream?'" Ashley asked jokingly. "I mean who wouldn't?" Other students nodded in approval.

Professor Christensen smiled then said "I want you to open a 'high-yield' savings account, a money market account, an online savings account, or other free account that offers a 'high' rate of return (around 1%), and then direct deposit your paycheck into this account. Look for banking institutions that also offer completely free checking accounts, mobile deposit, and zero minimum and opening balance requirements."

Justin interjected and asked "Where would I find a bank that does that? Don't most banks offer around 0.05%, but where do I find a bank to pay me about 1%? I don't want to tie my money up in a CD or something that prevents me from actually using my money."

"Great question!" Professor Christensen said as he smiled. "You actually are asking multiple questions, and I will only have the time to discuss some of your implied questions—I'll save the rest for a later class. But first, let me say: You are correct; you may want to avoid CDs right now. The rates are about what you would get with one of the high yield accounts I mentioned—but the problem is that you tie up your money for long periods of time. A high yield account is where you would save up your money to get your *Diamond*, or the goal that you are saving towards. You can at least pay for some of the sales tax by saving in a high yield savings account."

"How to find these accounts is by going to your bank and asking about a high yield savings accounts and/or money market accounts. You can also go to places like www.Money-Rates.com and www.nerdwallet.com to look for these accounts. Some places will require high initial deposits and high daily balances—you should avoid these places because they will most likely charge you a fee if you don't meet their minimums. Some sample companies might be www.ally.com, www.fidelity.com, or a regional credit union. Generally avoid institutions that require you to make a certain amount of purchases (most people end up spending more). Always ask about how fees work and how to avoid them. Any bank you choose should offer free checking options (you may need to have two accounts) and allow direct deposit."

"How do I set up direct deposit?" Tyler asked.

"Ask your employer, as each is different, but you will need your account number and routing number to your account," Professor Christensen responded. "All of this can be done with your employer. You can set up an account with a high yield savings account and then have your money automatically put into your account. If your bank offers it, you can do mobile deposit where an app takes a picture of your check using a Smartphone to deposit—this will allow you to avoid going to the bank and ensure that you get your money."

Justin remembered the long line he had to wait in at the bank. *Perfect! This will save me time and I don't have to worry about the check clearing in time or catching the bank during business hours. That is awesome.*

"Ask your HR department or supervisor about getting a 401(k), doing direct deposit, and remember the assignment to inquire about tuition assistance or reimbursement. Class dismissed."

When Justin got back to his apartment after work, he was surprised again. He'd gotten a letter from a scholarship he had applied to. Justin opened the letter and read,

Dear Mr. Murray,

    Congratulations! The committee has reviewed your application and has awarded a $1,000 scholarship if you are able to maintain at least a 3.3 GPA, starting with the present semester. The scholarship will be available to you at the beginning of next semester, assuming you are able to maintain credentials.

Keep up the good work! We wish you well.

Justin was taken aback. He had received another scholarship simply as a result of applying.

Chapter 8: Principles and Suggestions

1. Ask your HR department or supervisor about:

   a. Participating in a 401(k)

   b. Doing direct deposit

   c. Changing your W4 deductions to fit your situation—don't leave them at '0,' and

   d. Tuition assistance.

2. A 401(k) plan is free money when matched by an employer. If your employer doesn't offer a 401(k) plan, consider a Roth IRA. The habit of saving is important to establish.

   a. Consider investing in what are called *target date funds* (also called *life-cycle funds*).

   b. Have these contributions automatically made from your paycheck—you may not miss 5%.

   c. If done pre-tax, the money seems easier to bear.

3. Set up a high yield savings account that has the option of a free checking account (this will be used in a future chapter). You may need to set up two accounts—one for checking and the savings. Ensure that the savings account:

   a. Has a low opening balance (under $100)

   b. Has no minimum balance requirement

   c. Has at least a 0.75% annual percentage yield

   d. Is free (ask about how to avoid fees)

   e. Has online banking

   f. Has additional optional features including:

      i. Mobile deposit

      ii. Mobile fraud alerts

4. You can find a high yield savings account with your current bank (see the previous requirements for a high yield account) or by go-

ing to *www.Money-Rates.com* and *www.nerdwallet.com*. Some sample accounts might be:

  a. Ally Bank: *www.ally.com*

  b. Fidelity: *www.fidelity.com*

  c. A credit union in your area.

5. Change your tax deductions to be correct for your situation. A tax refund means that you offered the government an interest-free loan.

Chapter 8: Warnings and Avoidance

1. Avoid accounts that require you to spend certain amounts or make a certain amount of transactions.

2. Some high yield interest accounts may require you only to make a certain number of withdrawals—this is not a huge disadvantage; future chapters will discuss this.

3. Stock market can go down with your 401(k) plan. Speak with your financial advisor/employer's HR department.

Chapter 9: Making it Happen—Finances

Justin liked Professor Christensen's idea of being rewarded for getting money you earn anyway. For his part, Justin invariably paid off his credit card in full every month. His mom and grandpa had always made sure that that was the case. Since he was really quite impressed with what Professor Christensen said was available for payment options, he decided that he would put the professor's principles to the test.

Fixed Expenses and Fluctuating Expenses

At work, Justin got an email from Professor Christensen:

Class,

In addition to managing taxes, contacting the Human Resources rep about 401(k), and opening a high yield account, I want you to divide your expenses into fixed and fluctuating categories. We didn't get to it in class.

For example: rent, car insurance, health insurance, etc. are fixed expenses. Food, gasoline, fun, utilities, or anything else that varies is a fluctuating expense. Your cell phone depending upon your plan could be in either category. Basically, anything that doesn't change amounts over a repeatable period is a fixed expense.

Submit this along with the other assignments on the class website before our next class. See you then.

Sincerely,

Professor Christensen.

Justin started to work on homework. First though, Justin applied for another scholarship at work. Justin had written a paper for another class and he really liked the idea of turning every college paper and essay that he had written into a potential scholarship. It sort of gave him a monetary value for his papers, and it made them a lot more enjoyable to do. This helped him apply faster. It had been several weeks since Justin was awarded a scholarship, but he still trusted the assignment.

Justin decided that he would work on the banking section of the homework first. He went to his bank's website and chatted with an online customer service representative.

[Justin] Hello. I would like to find out about establishing a money market account.

[Rep] Yes, our bank has that. What do you want to know?

[Justin] Is there a minimum balance that is required?

[Rep] Do you mean to open an account, or for daily transactions?

[Justin] Both.

[Rep] There is a $10,000 minimum to open, and you must maintain a daily balance of at least $5,000.

[Justin] How many transactions are allowed?

[Rep] We allow six withdrawals and unlimited deposits each month.

[Justin] Just curious—why are the opening and daily balances so high when companies like Ally or ones found on Money-Rates.com and Nerd Wallet offer money market accounts for *no* minimum balances?

[Rep] Let me put it this way: our bank is in the business of making money. We only make money if certain balances are achieved.

Justin was a little taken aback. *Are you literally telling me that you are knowingly ripping me off? At whose expense are you 'achieving these balances?'* Justin kept his typing pleasant.

[Justin] How does Ally make money then?

[Rep] I don't know their business plan, but they have fewer buildings and less staff... you may not get as good of customer service.

[Justin] Can you match their savings products with lower opening minimums and no daily balance minimum—while still allowing me to get a higher interest rate?

[Rep] No.

[Justin] Can you give me any advantage of why I should choose the service you offer over the services by Ally or Fidelity or any other bank found from NerdWallet.com?

[Rep] You can have all of your banking in one place.

[Justin] I can link accounts to send and receive money automatically. Why would banking in one place help me, when you require such high minimum balances?

[Rep] Look, I don't make the rules. I just help people get what they need. We offer quality products to help our customers; if you don't want to take advantage of them that is fine.

[Justin] Okay, thanks.[30]

Every business is in the business of making money, Justin thought. *Else, why be in business? If that is how a representative of my bank does business, I think other businesses can at least treat me with courtesy. The representative's information might be only slightly accurate: while it might be true that companies like Ally or Fidelity have fewer buildings, the customer service might be just as good, if not better than, my current bank's customer service; plus I can do everything online.* Justin felt a little vindicated.

He went to *www.ally.com* and set up a high-yield savings account. He had to link his new account to his checking account. He did an initial funding which would take two business days to finalize, and he would not be able to withdraw the money for five business days after his initial deposit. However, Justin could use direct deposit with his wages immediately, to be deposited in his new money market account. He sent an e-mail to his boss asking if he could setup direct deposit, any available tuition assistance or reimbursement, and whether there was a 401(k) available to him. Justin had heard Kevin mention direct deposit a few times but had never really taken the time to set it up.

---

30 Similar to a real phone conversation the author had with a bank about fees. However, DO CHECK with your bank to see if they have competitive products.

On his way home, Justin stopped by Zion's bank because he had seen how they worked with small businesses and had a branch office at SSU. "I need to get some information about your savings and checking accounts for both individual accounts and small businesses."

"Sure thing," the woman teller replied, handing some pamphlets to Justin. "Our bank has some really good services for both personal accounts and small businesses."

Justin couldn't help but smile—remembering the chat session he had just finished. "Are there any fees for the checking accounts as long as I have a positive balance in the account?"

"We offer free checking for businesses and personal accounts. As long as you don't go over your balance, there is no fee—including no minimum balance or other fees, unless you use the ATM or order another service."

"That is good to know. Thanks," Justin said as he left.

Setting Up Direct Deposit and Changing Exemptions

At home, Justin checked his e-mail and found that Kevin, his boss, had answered. He described how to set up direct deposit and said that Justin needed to know his account and routing numbers. Kevin also provided a link to set this up. He said that SSU only allowed full-time employees to contribute to a 401(k) or get tuition covered by the university. So, those options weren't available to Justin. *This is a first... Professor Christensen's advice didn't work for me. At least I get direct deposit.*

Justin logged into his new high yield savings account with Ally and then clicked the link that Kevin had provided in his e-mail. He entered his banking information into his employee portal and saved it there. *No more going to the bank to cash my paycheck. This will be perfect!* Justin noticed that the form could process up to seven different accounts with direct deposit, allowing a portion of his paycheck to divide how he wanted. *Hmmm... I wonder how I could take advantage of that?*

While in his employee portal, Justin noticed a link that read "exemptions." *I wonder...* He clicked the link and found, not surprisingly, no exemptions. There was a questionnaire, and after answering it, Justin learned that he could rightfully claim a few exemptions, or deductible entries in the dependents' field, as allowed by law on his W-4 form.[31] After he clicked on "submit," the employee portal indicated that he would be saving some money by going to Ally bank and getting a bigger paycheck by not having tax deducted.

Benefits of Applying to Scholarships

The next day, Justin was checking his email and he noticed an email from a scholarship for which he had applied earlier in the semester. Justin had gotten used to these emails and letters; he had probably a dozen of them. The letters and emails would thank him for his submission and notify him that he had not been selected. Some would encourage him to apply again. It was kind of frustrating. Justin clicked the email and it read:

Congratulations Mr. Murray,

You have been awarded a $2,000 scholarship. The money has been sent to your campus' tuition department. You should see the money in the next 3-6 business days...

Justin was elated. *Holy cow! A 'free' $2,000 that is incredible.* Justin did a quick mental calculation: *I have spent less than 40 hours applying to scholarships: I was paid $50 PER HOUR?!!* Justin repeated. *That is amazing. Where else would I get paid that much—especially for just using my school essays and projects? Even though I have applied to 14 scholarships, just getting one makes it totally worth it.* Justin said a quick prayer and expressed gratitude for the scholarship.

Based on his previous experience, Justin knew that the surplus money would be offered to him from the tuition office as a check. Now that he had Ally for a bank, he wouldn't have to cash the check, as his phone had mobile deposit.

Justin went to the food court, hoping to run into Allison. On his way, Justin noticed an information booth that had a sign displaying an ad for 'Free Corn Maze Tickets.' (A farmer makes a maze in the dry stalks of his corn and invites people to come—usually for a cost.) While he wasn't interested in the promotion, the tickets seemed fun.

---

31 Every W-4 form has a questionnaire for adding up legal dependents and exemptions. Please check your employer's payroll department (usually HR) so that you are not deducted more than is owed you.

Justin then went to the food court; he was in luck! Allison was at the register.

"Hey, Justin," Allison said with a smile.

"How's it going?" Justin asked.

"Fine," said Allison.

"Could I get a small loaf of wheat bread with some honey butter?" Justin asked.

"Sure thing," Allison responded. As she was getting the bread, she asked. "Have you started on the homework yet?"

"Yeah," he answered. "Yesterday, I opened a high yield savings account, started direct deposit; and changed my W4 allotments."

"Good job!" said Allison. "You're almost done."

"I just got another scholarship. I can't believe how much I was offered; I added up my time spent applying to all the scholarships and I made over $50 per hour."

"That's crazy, isn't it?" Allison commented.

Justin then asked Allison how *she* was doing on the homework.

401(k) Benefits and Tuition Reimbursement

"You're not going to believe this," Allison said. "I checked at work if they have a 401(k) program and any tuition assistance, and I was surprised: they had both."

"Wait– the school doesn't have a 401(k) program. I checked," Justin said.

"I meant," said Allison, correcting him, "my other job at the hotel. I'm working two jobs."

"Oh," said Justin.

Allison continued. "It turns out they offer 100% 401(k) matching up to 4% of my total paycheck. And they offer $1,000 of tuition reimbursement every six months, for their tuition assistance program, after I've worked there for a minimum of two months. Since I started the job in the summer, I'm just barely eligible. I spoke with my human resources contact and started the reimbursement process for summer classes. Can you believe that?!"

"That's great!" said Justin.

"I get summer classes reimbursed from tuition reimbursement—plus, an additional 4% of my paycheck if I start contributing to my 401(k) plan!" Allison said excitedly.

"So did you?" Justin asked with joking curiosity.

"Of course!" replied Allison. "I had the handout in my backpack when I called my human resources contact, and I asked about target date funds. The HR representative said those were standard. He sent me to the company intranet to see the forms for both the 401(k) and the tuition reimbursement. I filled them out electronically and sent them in. Starting next paycheck, I'll be contributing a full 6%, to make an even 10%—I figured with the $1,000 dollars for tuition reimbursement, I was able to route some of my paycheck to be saved—especially when it's matched by my employer."

"That was nice."

"It sure was!" Then Allison handed Justin his warm bread. "Here's your bread."

They had been engrossed in their conversation and didn't realize they were holding up the line. Justin paid and left to eat his bread.

"Real quick," Justin said.

"Yeah. What is it?" Allison responded.

"I got some tickets to go to a corn maze and wondered if you'd like to go with me this Saturday at 6 p.m."

"Sounds fun, I'll see you then," Allison said handing Justin his receipt.

That afternoon at work, Justin quickly submitted another scholarship. He wanted in on this free-money deal both he and Allison had gotten. *Allison got hooked up*, Justin thought. *I wish I could have a job like that.* He was a little envious of her getting tuition reimbursement and 401(k) money. *Free money. Hmmm, that sounds even better than free pizza.* Justin was grateful that his job at least allowed him to do his homework—and he had gotten $2,000. Justin then sent an e-mail to Bob, the program advisor whom he had met when he first came to SSU, asking if there were any additional scholarships being offered for his major. He was excited to start earning interest on his money while he saved up for next semester's tuition and going to Machu Picchu.

Corn Maze Chats—Principles Yield Good Things

At the corn maze, Justin and Allison tried to see how lost they could get in the maze—then how they would find which direction to go. As they walked they talked about different things. After a while, Allison asked Justin, "What have you enjoyed about our class and how has it helped you?"

Justin was a little taken aback at the talk of finances on a date, but he answered willingly enough. "Well, my mom and my grandpa always stressed paying off credit cards in full. I have more money coming in than going out, and I'm not too flashy with my money– I just basically pay for a car and food, and save up for tuition—though I do have to admit that Professor Christensen's class has helped a lot, with the scholarships and the money management."

"I know what you mean," said Allison. "It's been a huge blessing in *my* life too. I have received two scholarships out of the 11 I have applied for—plus the Pell Grant."

"Good for you! I've received four scholarships."

"Still, that was money you didn't have to earn," she said. "How many scholarships have your applied for?"

"Twenty-one," Justin said.

"Whoa! How'd you apply to so many?" Allison asked.

"I made a system to help me apply faster," he replied.

"Could you teach me later how you did that?"

"Sure. When school started my dad's company almost had layoffs, and he couldn't pay for my schooling. I was really worried, but now I am getting more money coming to me than if he actually had paid for it—thanks to Professor Christensen's class. What have you learned from the class?"

"My dad taught me to live within my means, but I really like automatic saving and debt prevention. I have also been enjoying the real estate and business concepts.[32] These have really helped towards my goals."

"What's your savings goal?" Justin asked.

"I want to buy a property and go on a trip to China. I've always dreamt of Beijing. What's your goal?"

"Buy a property, graduate without student loans or credit card debt, and go on a trip to Machu Picchu. I've wanted to go since I was in Ecuador," he answered enthusiastically.

"Agreed. It's so much easier since I started doing my finances automatically," Allison said. "Previously, I didn't have any real hope; Beijing was just a wish, but now I have a plan and it feels so good that I'll go there debt free—plus I am thinking I will get points from getting a rewards credit card with a lot of points upfront."

"I know what you mean," said Justin. "My life is easier when I don't have to worry about paying my bills myself."

They continued talking and Allison said, "I'm working a swing shift at a hotel. I work Monday to Friday. That lets me get my homework done."

"Wait," said Justin. "Every time we've met up for study groups—how could you come if you had a swing shift?"

"My work's really flexible, as long as it's not the holiday season. I can make a request for time off for a study group. Plus I only work 4 days a week, so I can move my schedule around as long as I give advance notice," Allison explained.

"Gotcha," said Justin. "That's cool. How long have you been doing the hotel job?"

"Well, the hotel is really just for college, since it lets me work on my homework at the same time."

"Yeah, me too!" said Justin. "I work at the computer lab, and that's kind of how *my* job is."

---

32 The reader can get the Author's books entitled '*Winning the Money Game in College*' — '*Real Estate*' and '*Business*' books at *www.CollegeCashChampion.com.*

"Oh, really?" said Allison. "That's awesome!"

Justin talked a little bit more about being a lab aid; he really enjoyed doing his homework while getting paid.

Allison agreed, "Yeah, I really enjoy that part of the hotel. That's why I work at the fast-food café too."

"What do you mean?" asked Justin.

"Well," Allison said, "at the end of the day they have leftovers, and the leftovers are offered to the employees at a huge discount. I try to stick to the healthier stuff; things like salads, baked potatoes, soup, and the grilled chicken, or whatever, always come in handy."

Justin nodded in agreement.

"However," Allison added, "I may soon quit the fast food job and change my shift at work; scholarships and business money have helped a lot."

Chapter 9: Principles and Suggestions

4. Start earning money on your income by setting up a 'high yield' savings account.

5. Check with your employer about direct deposit, tuition reimbursement, 401(k) contributions, and W4 tax allocation.

6. Applying to multiple scholarships is like getting $10 to $500 per hour. They really do pay off.

Chapter 9: Warnings and Avoidance

1. Don't get discouraged if it seems that applying to scholarships is not working out, or if every principle taught cannot be applied to you. Become aware of what is available to you and use that to your advantage.

2. The biggest problem that most people face is either not knowing about a solution, or not taking action to implement it. You now know many of the solutions; how are you doing about implementing them?

Chapter 10: Money Channels

Justin was excited to attend class on Wednesday. He and Allison were talking when class began. Allison had similar success—she was awarded a Pell Grant by applying to FAFSA, had some scholarships, tuition reimbursement, a 401(k), and now was saving money in a high yield account.

Professor Christensen started to address the class.

Handout Excerpt: Setting Yourself Up to Win

"Has anyone seen the TV game show: '*The Price is Right*'?"

"Who hasn't?" Malcolm asked.

"Has anyone seen the game *Plinko*?" Professor Christensen continued. A few students had. "Can anyone explain the game?"

Tyler made the attempt: "*Plinko* is a game where contestants drop a circular disk on a vertical board that has pegs on it. The disk will fall either to the left or right when it hits the peg. At the bottom the disk goes into different slots that offer different levels of prizes. The contestants try to start the disk in the right track so it hits the biggest prize as it falls."

"Very well said!" Professor Christensen commented. "I want to show you a system to place your money automatically into the right slot—so you don't have to think about it."

"How is that going to work?" Ashley asked, curiously.

"The good news," Professor Christensen said, "is that we have already set up many of the parts needed. By now most of the class has found his or her *Bubblegum-Diamond-Thieves*, allocated paychecks to a high yield account, adjusted taxes, added income sources to your life, and you should have at least one fun goal to work towards. Additionally, you should have added up your fixed and fluctuating expenses. Let's add a few more parts and you'll be set. I think you are going to like this next part."

At the sound of the assignment of fixed and fluctuating expenses, Justin remembered he had forgotten to do that part of the assignment. *What! I completely forgot. Aww snap. Professor Christensen is going to give me a '0.' This is going to kill my grade.*

Professor Christensen continued interrupting Justin's thoughts, "What if I offered you a coupon that would give you up to a 15% discount on your tuition? Would you use it?"

"I'd sure jump on that," Malcolm said. "But what school is going to offer any discount on tuition?"

529 Savings Plans—A Fast Way to Save Big

"Has anyone heard of a 529 Education Savings Plan?" the professor asked.

A few people kind of shrugged.

"For example, the Utah Education Savings Plan (UESP) offers a 5% state income tax credit. If you were to open an account, put your tuition money in, then take it out, you could use it for any college or trade school and get 5% credit on your state taxes. This means that if you were to open a 529 UESP, you could get an instant discount on your taxes (or taxes of your parents or guardian—the account owner) for contributing your 529 Savings plan. As a bonus: any money grows tax free on all interest and gains, so you won't get taxed as long as the money is used for qualified expenses—so if your money grows 10-40% you won't be taxed on the gains."

"What are qualified expenses?" Allison asked.

Professor Christensen advanced the slide. It read

- You can have your money grow tax free as long as you use it for qualified expenses: Tuition, lab/class fees, books, room and board (place to stay and limited food to eat).

- If expenses are for non-qualified purchases, you will be taxed and penalized on the gains.

Here is what you should check with a 529 Education Savings Plan (different states have different features with their plan):

- Where does the plan allow the beneficiary to use the money (what types of institutions)?

- What do I need to do to get the money out and have it count as a qualified expense?

- Will I be reimbursed, have the money go to my school, or will I need to get a special debit card/checkbook to get my money?

- Who is the guardian/custodian of the money and what are their rules?

- Do you get any state tax credits for investing in a 529 ESP in your state?

- What are the fees associated with the 529 savings plan I choose (they vary from state to state/plan)?

- What investment funds are available in the plan?

"Clark Howard described 'Utah's plan as the single best plan in the country.' Even if you are not from Utah, you can still benefit from this plan because of the low fees and flexibility," Professor Christensen said. "I invite you to see Clark Howard's guide at: *http://www.clark-howard.com/news/clark-howard/education/clarks-529-guide/nFZS/*.

"Also, I would recommend visiting this website: *www.saving-forcollege.com*, as they will give a comparison of what the benefits of the various 529 savings plans are among the states. I recommend that you check out their saving vs. borrowing calculators; you can easily save 32% or more by saving for college rather than borrowing money."

"Just by opening a UESP and paying your tuition, books, and rent with a 529 savings plan, you can potentially get a 5% discount for not having to pay Utah state income tax. Additionally, you can save by not having to pay tax on your gains—plus later on this will become very helpful when we talk about real estate. If you go to a different school in another state, other states will have different, but similar, resources available."

"You mean that we can get a 5% discount on tuition, books, and rent just for putting money in, then immediately paying from school from the Utah Education Savings Plan?" Ashley asked.

"It will depend on how much you pay in income tax, but the short answer is: pretty much, yes—if your 529 savings plan allows it." Professor Christensen replied. "The tax credit goes to the account owner when taxes are filed, but this is a great opportunity to get a tax credit—which acts as a gain, in preventing a loss. It works out as a great strategy."

"I am so doing that," Ashley said.

"Keep in mind the limits of what school costs, because unless it is a qualified expense, you will be penalized. This is just another game that the IRS requires that we play," Professor Christensen responded. "This is all just part of the complexity of the present tax code. It does require some hoops to be jumped through, but the rewards are worth it."

"There are more parts to the system, but let me give you an overview of where we are going to go." Professor Christensen advanced the slide to show:

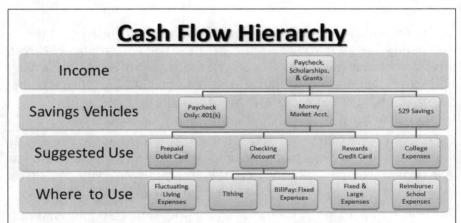

"The point is that money automatically goes where it needs to be. You determine in advance how much you need and put it there. You can make adjustments if needed. There are three more parts that we need to talk about: BillPay, a rewards credit card, and a prepaid-debit card. But for now, let's focus on the flow of cash—when you get it, where it goes and how to do this automatically."

"Paychecks and scholarships go to a money market or high-yield savings account, 529 Savings Plan, and if your work provides it, a 401(k) plan. The money market keeps your emergency fund, or a freedom continuation plan, savings for your future expenses, and your goals and dreams money.

"Money flows from one account to another, automatically," Professor Christensen said, "but you only will use one part of the system for everyday expenses—and that is your prepaid-debit card. This will prevent you from impulsively buying, and it prevents you from having to keep track of every penny that a lot of budgeting concepts/software have you do. This is similar to the envelope system that many people use, but rather than having to keep refilling your envelopes each month, it happens automatically—plus you don't have to carry wads of cash around with you. You just have to commit that you will live only on the money in this prepaid-debit card. If you spend too much on junk, you had better be willing to eat a lot of rice."

"Use a rewards credit card and BillPay—I will explain this in a moment, for fixed expenses, and pay the credit card off in full every month. This is one of the key parts; you use a rewards card for fixed expenses (amounts that don't change each month—cell phone, rent, insurance, etc.), and a prepaid-debit card for fluctuating expenses (food, gas, fun, entertainment, etc.). The prepaid-debit card I will explain more in depth a little bit later, but let me explain credit cards first."

Benefits of a Good Rewards Credit Card

"Get a rewards card of your choice: cash, points, or miles. Generally free rewards cards are best unless you get a huge bonus upfront. Use this card to pay off your fixed expenses. You may also use this card for future expenses that are large purchases such as tuition and rent."

"Did anyone put a trip on the goals that you wanted for your diamond prize?" Several people raised their hands.

"Great. Let me give you a tip that will greatly help you: Get a rewards credit card that offers you a large amount of miles upfront (say 30,000 to 50,000 points) if you spend several thousand in a few months' time. Pay tuition with this credit card, and earn a free trip. Check with your 529 savings plan and see if you can get reimbursed for a qualified expense, saving money on state taxes and free gains. Pay the card off in full from money in your 529 savings plan or checking account. You just earned a free trip or more. Use this as your rewards credit card when making large purchases. You may want to consider getting two credit cards: a free rewards card that you will use for your fixed expenses, and a paid credit card for large purchases like tuition that offers an enormous amount of points upfront for making tuition happen."

Justin realized that he could get a lot of points just for paying for tuition. *Machu Picchu might be closer than I think.*

"Great!" Malcolm blurted out. "Now you tell me after I have already paid this semester's tuition."

"If you have already paid this semester's tuition, keep it in mind for next semester, or see if the tuition office will let you pay with your credit card now and get a check back," the professor said.

How to Find a Good Rewards Credit Card

"Good," said the professor. "Now for the rewards credit cards.[33] Generally avoid card offers that come in the mail or on campus; avoid credit cards that are specific to any one merchant—both the cards in the mail and the merchant cards tend to have the most penalties and highest interest, often with the least amount of flexibility."

"Get credit cards that give you more advantage than what it costs for the card. Paying $19 to get a 1%-back card is not that great an idea, as you need to spend $1,900 before you start seeing any profits. . However, if you were to be offered 5% for the categories in your fixed-spending bucket, then you would only need to spend $380 be-

---

33 The author realizes that getting a good credit card depends on good credit. For more suggestions on improving credit, please see the author's book entitled: *Winning the Money Game in College: Real Estate.*

fore you start seeing 5% rewards. . Still, *paying* to receive rewards doesn't always benefit you, as the credit card company may change its rewards program, and you would be out the cost of the rewards card, plus, lose the interest you could have earned on purchases. Paying for a credit card generally makes sense if you are getting high rewards upfront, such as two round-trip plane tickets or something similar. You can find several great free and paid credit cards on CreditCards.com or Credit.com by going to *www.creditcards.com* or *www.credit.com/ credit-cards/*. Be sure to read the terms and ensure that rewards are not just *temporary* or *introductory*."

"Any questions?" Professor Christensen asked.

"My apartment won't accept credit cards without a fee. Is it worth it to get the rewards?" Allison asked.

"Generally, no; don't use your credit card if there will be a transactional fee charged to you. If the merchant doesn't accept credit cards, or if you can't pay automatically without a penalty, then for majority of cases I would say no, don't use a credit card. If you'd like to automate and the place you need to pay won't accept your credit card without a penalty, I have something better in mind," Professor Christensen said. "But before I introduce that concept, any other questions?"

Justin raised his hand and asked "Why did you suggest using a pre-paid-debit card instead of a regular debit card, cash, or another credit card for the fluctuating expenses?

"I'm glad you asked. Thank you for the reminder!" Professor Christensen said. "If you use a prepaid-debit card it is more secure, but acts like cash. You can never go over the balance. Most debit cards will allow you to go over your account balance and then charge you fees and interest—with no warning of being over the limit. A credit card makes it really easy to spend more than you wanted. A prepaid-debit card allows you to determine in advance what you want your fluctuating expenses to be, not exceed your predetermined limits, and have security if it is ever lost or stolen. You can get a prepaid-debit card by:

- Contacting your checking account company and asking that your account deny the charge if it goes over the available balance in your checking account—you must specifically request this feature to be added. (Then you must transfer into your checking account the money that you need. Check with your employer about splitting your paycheck to have part of the money go into your checking account and part into your high yield savings account.)

- Or by getting a reloadable prepaid-debit card from a site like *www.creditcards.com* or *www.credit.com/credit-cards/*."

"You mean banks will charge me if I go over my account balance if I use a regular debit card?" Ashley asked.

"Both fees and interest," Professor Christensen said. "This is kind of sad, but true."

"That is so stupid," Allison said. "Why don't they just deny the charge? It seems that they're only after your money."

"True," Professor Christensen said, "but this is where the idea comes that I referenced with you earlier."

"What's your idea?" Allison asked inquisitively.

How to Use BillPay—Automatically Paying Bills

"Has anyone heard of BillPay?" The Professor asked.

A few people raised their hands.

"Well," said the professor, "for those of you who may not know what it is, BillPay is generally a free service through your bank that will send out a certified check to either an individual or an institution, to arrive by a date that you select."

"If businesses will take checks, this is where BillPay comes in handy. You simply submit the name of the business, as well as your name and account number with that business, and your bank will print all the information on the check when it's sent. You will set up whatever reoccurring schedule you need for each check: monthly, quarterly, annually, or just once. So with BillPay, you can have your bills paid automatically."

"Has anyone ever used BillPay?" Professor Christensen asked. A couple of people raised their hands.

"Well, good! Some of you are familiar with the process."

"When you combine all the parts of a high yield savings account, 401(k), 529 Educational Savings Plan (ESP), rewards credit card, and prepaid-debit card, this system does at least four things for you: One, it pays your bills on time — automatically. Two, it builds your credit history and credit score. Three, it offers you rewards of your choosing, either points, miles, or cash for your largest expenses such as tuition. Four, it allows you to get free money and save for the future."

"Ultimately, what happens is that you pay most of your fixed expenses on a credit card that offers rewards, only using BillPay for those fixed expenses that don't accept credit cards or won't allow you to make repeated transactions. Thereby you earn rewards from your rewards credit card without having to do anything extra except pay your bills on time. You no longer have to worry about payment of your fixed bills."

"Of course, you must notify BillPay of the date you want the check to arrive at the recipient. Bear in mind that it usually takes five business days for the bank to make a check. So, knowing the date you would like the check to be delivered, count backwards six business days so that the funds can settle, and that will be the day that you'll need to have money in your account. However, I recommend an extra two-day cushion.

"This seems kind of confusing," Ashley said. "Isn't there a step by step method?"

"I'm glad that you asked." Professor Christensen said as he advanced the slide and announced: Process for paycheck. This will be a slight repeat, but I want to make sure that you get this. It is crucial for you to understand this plan."

"The key here is to have money flow automatically; set it up once and you are done worrying about where your money is going," the professor said. "Think of each step as a slice of your total income; by the time it gets to less important things, the important ones have already been taken care of. The point is not to waste your money on useless things, but to get what you really want."

Professor Christensen had everyone turn to the correct page in their handout *Setting Yourself Up to Win*[34] and read a quote:

---

34 Available at *www.CollegeCashChampion.com*.

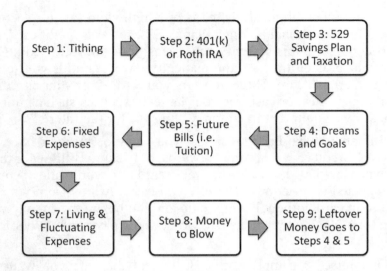

I can't think of a single thing I purchased on a credit card during my late teen and college years that I kept later in life. You need to spend wisely and set boundaries. Credit cards aren't free money, so don't treat them that way.[35]

"This is why I want you to pick a big dream," the professor said. "I want you to spend *on purpose*. This blogger talked about spending frivolously and the tens of thousands of dollars it cost him. When you have a goal that you want bad enough, you can ask yourself: 'Do I want this small insignificant item or my goal? Do I want bubblegum or a diamond?'"

"Think of each dollar as a seed. You can either *eat* the seed or *plant* the seed. Truthfully, you will need to do both—figuratively eating some seeds and planting the rest. If your life depended on these seeds, you would use them very carefully. You would plant some and use some, but you wouldn't just throw the seeds into the fire. You would take care of them as best you could by planning and taking care of your seeds.[36] Let's do the same thing with your money: create a plan and spend your

---

35Howard, Clark. "Clark's 529 Guide." www.clarkhoward.com. Accessed April 19, 2014. www.clark-howard.com/news/clark-howard/education/clarks-529-guide/nFZS/.

36 Hansen, Mark Victor, and Robert G. Allen. *The One Minute Millionaire: The Enlightened Way to Wealth*. New York: Three Rivers Press, 2009.

money wisely. What I will call Pre-steps are preparation steps, or steps to take to prepare to do the rest."

"Pre-Step 1: Make a really fun goal that you want, and a basic plan to work towards."

"Pre-Step 2: Sort your present expenses into three categories: Fixed expenses (expenses that don't change, i.e., rent), fluctuating expenses (ones that change, i.e., grocery bill), future bills (i.e., tuition)."

"Pre-Step 3: Determine if your expenses are bringing you closer to your goals (diamonds) or are unnecessary (bubblegum); decide what bubblegum you do want to keep (i.e. $10 per month to be with friends), but keep it minimal. Eliminate expenses that you would be willing to give up in order to get your goal (i.e., reduce fast food, sell a car—no more gasoline or insurance, or buy in bulk). Would you rather have bubblegum or diamonds?"

"Pre-Step 4: Find out if your fixed expenses take a credit card *without a fee* and can bill you automatically. If they don't, inquire about their address to mail a payment. (While inquiring, it might be helpful to find a mailing address to send a check if they don't accept credit cards without a fee.)"

"Pre-Step 5: Open a money market account or high yield savings account, checking account, rewards credit card, and free and reloadable prepaid-debit card that you can put a reoccurring balance on each month."

"Do we pay off each of those steps in the graphic completely?" Allison asked.

"Each step gets a slice of your total income—either a percentage or a fixed amount. I put the items in order of payment priority. Some items like your future tuition you may not be able to pay off, but saving up for it over time helps lots."

"'Kay. That helps clarify things for me," Allison said. Professor Christensen returned to the graphic to explain.

"Step 1: Decide to pay your tithing. Tithing works."

"Step 2: Allocate an amount to go to your 401(k) or IRA, before the government takes *its* bite. Even if it is $20 per month; this will allow you to get any matching that your employer offers, and will help get you in the habit of saving."

"What if my employer doesn't offer a 401(k) plan?" Ashley asked.

"Consider participating in a Roth IRA—which takes funds after tax, but grows tax free," Professor Christensen said.

Professor Christensen read the next slide: "Step 3 (multiple steps):

- Allocate your W4 to have the correct amount of exemptions to prevent being over-taxed—speak to your accountant and HR representative.

- (This sub-step fits in both steps 3 and 5.) Decide to open a 529 Savings Plan. Use it to save money for school expenses. The Utah ESP is a great recommendation.

- Open a money market account such as with Ally or Fidelity that pays about 1% return. Have your money and/or paycheck go automatically into your money market account—without going to the bank to cash your check using direct deposit with your employer."

  o Alternatively, if your employer doesn't allow direct deposit, inquire if your bank has a money market account AND an app for your Smartphone that deposits checks with pictures.

"Step 4: Start living your dreams. What do you really want? Find out how much it costs, and then set aside money until you get it (i.e., something like $50 per month)."

"Wouldn't it be better to just buy what you want and pay it off so you can enjoy it longer?" Tyler asked.

"Great question," Professor Christensen said. "What's something you want?"

"I want a new laptop—in fact I need one for school, and it'd be nice to have to watch movies with."

"A new laptop costs now about $250 to $2,500 depending on type and style. If you were to purchase this on a credit card—even if you paid it off in 5 years, you would spend 1.4 to 1.9 times as much on your computer. What are some things Tyler could do while he is saving up to buy a computer?" Professor Christensen asked the class.

"Borrow a friend's."

"Use the campus computers."

"If you don't need to have a brand new one, there are plenty of used computers for under $100 available on Craigslist.com or VendAnything.com."

"Great ideas!" Professor Christensen said. "If you absolutely must have a new one, why not save up and wait till right after Thanksgiving on Friday-Monday of that week? Stores cut prices on many items by 20-80% and you can get a new computer for hundreds less. But even more important than getting a deal, you'll have purchased it debt free by saving up. There'll be no dragon looming over your life because you haven't paid your bills. You won't have a constant worry and you won't end up being 'a day late and a dollar short.'"

"I had never thought of those ideas." Tyler said.

"Another problem with buying before you have the money is: when do you stop? When do you stop buying things before you have the money? If you buy a laptop, it could become a habit and then soon you might buy clothing, MP3s, shoes, and even groceries on credit. Why don't you look at the handout *Setting Yourself Up to Win* for further clarification?" Professor Christensen suggested. He advanced the slide.

"Step 5: Similar to Step 4, if you know you have big expenses coming, such as next semester's tuition, save up for it now. I highly recommend that you use a 529 Education Savings Plan, and the Utah Education Savings Plan allows you to contribute automatically. This may also save you on state income taxes, but allow your money to grow tax free."

"If you happen to have scholarships available to you, I recommend that you check with the school's tuition office about what happens if you overpay tuition. Many times, if there's a surplus of funds you can have the money returned to you. For example, if you have a scholarship that covers tuition, and you were to pay with a 529 Savings plan, you would get to keep the money from the scholarship and get the tax and savings benefits from using your 529 savings plan—a double win."

"Other bills can and should be saved up for in advance. This makes your financial life cheaper and easier by not having to pay for items over and over again by paying interest and penalties. Save for your bills before purchase."

"Next, let's automate where your paycheck goes. Make your life simple. Set things up once and you're done. You review periodically, but mostly you just set up automatic payments and let your bills get taken care of automatically. That way, you'll *never have* a late payment or interest. Automate your financial life. The more complex people's systems are, the more unlikely it is that they'll have financial success. This is why I suggest automating your payments."

"That'd be nice," Malcolm said.

Professor Christensen smiled.

"Step 6: Add up all your fixed expenses—things like cell phone, rent, insurance, and other expenses that don't change from month to month, or year to year—and pay them all with a designated rewards credit card used only for your fixed expenses. I'll explain how to do this in a moment."

"Step 7: Get a *prepaid-debit* or credit card that will only allow you to use the specific amount. You can find these cards at CreditCards. com or Credit.com. Decide on what you need for fluctuating expenses: food, gas, and fun. Use only this card. Leave your other cards at home. You can spend your money on whatever you want, but know this: if you use your money for the month on a lot of worthless junk, you will be eating Ramen Noodles for the rest of the month."

"Step 8: Go blow some money. If you have already allocated your money and paid your expenses, go have some fun using your prepaid-debit card. Decide in advance how much you will spend each month on everyday expenses; if there is money left on the prepaid-debit card, you get to use it. This is a reward for managing your money well."

"Step 9: If you want your future goal more than blowing money, put the remainder of the money back towards your goals in steps 4 and 5."

Ashley raised her hand. "That seems kind of complex. Professor Christensen, exactly how do we do this? I mean, I can't purchase expensive software."

"I wouldn't ask you to increase your spending," Professor Christensen reassured, "but I am glad you asked. There is a great, free service to track your money through *www.Mint.com* or *Check.me*, which offers a pretty neat way to manage your money. Simply go to www. mint.com or https://check.me/ and sign up for a secure account. This will help you to find out where your money is going, but we still need to automate payments.

"This is your assignment," Professor Christensen said as he advanced the slide. He read aloud:

Chapter 10: Principles and Suggestions

1. Pick a really fun, big goal that you have been dreaming about purchasing. Write it down and pick a date when you will obtain your item. Then write the amount of money you need to save each month in order to get that goal. Keep this money away from your checking account by keeping it in your high yield savings account or money market account.

2. Read over the handout *Setting Yourself Up to Win* available on *www.CollegeCashChampion.com* and write a one-page summary of the entire handout. Use this in the next step.

3. Automate everything financial in your life. Set up your paycheck and scholarships to be deposited directly into your bank account.

4. Get a free rewards credit card if you don't already have one. See if you can get one by going to *www.creditcards.com* or *www.credit. com/credit-cards/* and applying online. Use this card exclusively for fixed payments.

   a. **<u>PAY THE CARD OFF IN FULL</u>** each month, automatically, by contacting the credit card company and linking it to your checking account or high-yield or money market account. (Keep in mind that you are allowed a limited amount of transactions with a money market or high-yield account, and the credit card withdrawal counts as one withdrawal.)

   b. You may want to get a second high rewards credit card that offers you a lot of points, cash, or trip upfront. Get and use this high rewards card near the start of a semester to get a huge reward for paying tuition. (Often as part of the big rewards, you need to spend a few thousand dollars in a short time frame; hence the recommendation to get it right before tuition is due.)

5. For individuals and/or companies that either do not accept credit cards or charge a fee to use them, use BillPay to send them a recurring check from your checking account.

6. Get a reloadable, prepaid-debit card that only allows you to spend what you fund on the card (this works mostly like cash, except you will not accidentally exceed a limit and get charged with a fee, as you would with a debit card).

7. Find what you can eliminate from your expenses:

    a. Selling your car and using a bike and public transportation

    b. Setting a check card for entertainment

    c. Using coupons and promotion codes

    d. Going to Redbox instead of the movie theater

    e. Reducing or eliminating eating out

    f. Getting a job closer to where you live

    g. Buying in bulk

    h. Changing apartments (to be nearer school and work, or to be cheaper)

Chapter 10: Warnings and Avoidance

1. Never cash a check at a check cashing location—they charge 3-9% of your check. Use your, or the check issuer's, bank instead.

2. Get rewards credit cards to pay off fixed and fluctuating expenses. WARNINGS:

    a. Link the credit cards to your checking account or you won't be able to automatically pay the balance (call the credit card company for directions).

    b. Make sure that the credit card has at least 20 days for a grace period.

c. Pay the credit card off in full every month on the same day each month; if you don't, you will be charged interest, penalties, and may lose your rewards.

d. Get a rewards credit card for fixed expenses, and a pre-paid credit card for your monthly expenses. Only carry the pre-paid card with you.

3. Avoid paying for your goals and dreams until you have the cash. Things get cheaper when you save, but get more expensive when you buy on credit.

4. While you are encouraged to "blow" some of your money, don't overdo it. Plan in advance what you can realistically afford, without sacrificing your goals, dreams, and other expenses, and then only spend that amount. Find cheaper ways to do the same thing. Instead of going to a newly released movie, wait 3 months, get it for under $2 and have a party at a neighbor's apartment.

5. Avoid getting credit cards from department stores and credit card offers in the mail. Most of the time these have really steep penalties, interest, and other charges. Additionally, they don't really help build your credit.

"Any questions?" the professor asked when he had finished reading the slide. No hands went up. "Well, no class until next week. In the meantime, apply to another scholarship and automate your financial life."

The bell rang, and Justin was amazed that Professor Christensen could both teach them how to spend on purpose *and* be so good at timing the bell. However, Justin was wondering about how his grade would fair because he forgot to do part of the assignment.

Chapter 11: Automatic Money Success

After class, Justin went up to Professor Christensen. "I was wondering about the assignment to add up my fixed and fluctuating expenses… I had so many things going on, I completely forgot. Could I still get credit for the assignment if I do it now?"

"The good news is, Justin," Professor Christensen empathetically, "you will still be able to do the assignment. In fact, it is still required for the money channels assignment. The bad news is that for that part of the assignment, you will be getting a '0.' If you had an illness or school-excused absence, I could've been lenient, but since you didn't, unfortunately, this assignment will be a '0.' I have to be fair to the other class members who submitted the assignment on time. You know the class rules, but don't worry, you will still be able to get an 'A' in the class if you don't let this happen again and submit every assignment on time. You are doing really well. *Don't let a simple slip up destroy everything you have worked towards.* Learn from it, make corrections, and do better here on out."

Justin left feeling both discouraged at missing an assignment, and glad that Professor Christensen took the time to pay him a compliment. *I guess I deserve that '0.' But it still irks me that I missed a simple assignment. Professor Christensen was really nice about it—he even paid me a compliment, but I definitely don't want to make that mistake again.*

Justin went online and looked at his finances. *Hey, if I put my fixed expenses like my cell phone, rent, my part of the Internet fees, that all have fixed costs, on a rewards credit card or BillPay I can maximize my return on my credit card. Do I really need everything I buy or subscribe to?* Justin was remembering the *Bubblegum-Diamond Thief* concept. Justin took Professor Christensen's advice and canceled unnecessary subscriptions.

Getting a Good Credit Card

At this point, Justin was gathering information for his finances rather than setting up an automated system—that part would come after he finalized his credit card. He looked at his credit card bill and spotted a couple of things he had not noticed before: The company charged him an annual fee of $23.00 and offered him 1.2% rewards.

Let me see... Justin opened the calculator on the computer and typed in the break-even equation:. *I have to spend almost $2,000 before I can even start making a profit!!! That's ridiculous.* He navigated his browser to *www.creditcards.com* and *www.credit.com/credit-cards/* and did a quick credit card search. He soon found that there were many free rewards cards available. *Miles, points, or cash: which do I want?* One of the cards was a free version of the card he already had. Justin jotted it down, along with a few of the other offers, and then got ready to leave the lab. Erin would be there soon to take his place.

When Erin arrived, Justin packed up his stuff and left. On his way back to his car, Justin pulled out his credit card, dialed the number on the back of it, and asked to speak to a manager from his card company.

The attendant who answered said, "A supervisor is not available. You will have to call again later."

Justin remembered what Professor Christensen's handout had said that credit card companies were required to have a supervisor available.

"Excuse me," he interrupted, "isn't it a fact that by law you're required to have a supervisor available at all times during business operating hours?" Justin was more nervous than confident. He really didn't have much to go on and was hoping that the receptionist wouldn't call him on the fact, because he didn't know—he was just relying on what the professor had said in his handout.

"Let me check if one might be available," the representative said. "I can transfer you to Mr. Sullivan."[37]

---

37 Receptionists have the power to say 'no' but rarely have the power to say 'yes.' Speak to a supervisor.

"Thanks," said Justin, relieved at not being called out.

After a few minutes, the voice on the other end said, "Hello, this is Peter Sullivan. Whom do I have the pleasure of speaking with?"

Justin gave his name and verified his credit card information.

"What can I do for you?" Mr. Sullivan asked.

"I was wondering if I could be switched to a *free* rewards credit card," Justin responded. "I'm on the paid version of the card, but I would like to have the free version."

"The free version has half the rewards points," Mr. Sullivan said.

"I know," said Justin, "but right now I have to spend over $1,900 before I see a penny of rewards anyway. I won't lose any of the points I *have* acquired, will I?"

"There is no loss of accrued points if you convert to the free card,"[38] Mr. Sullivan said, in a tone that conveyed he knew what Justin was referring to.

"Great, may I keep the same credit card number?"

"We will send you a new card that is designed differently, but your credit card number will remain the same," Mr. Sullivan replied.

"Let me give you my updated address." Justin provided his new address and then confirmed the conversion of the card. He thanked Mr. Sullivan for his time and ended the call.

After hanging up the phone, Justin was amazed that it had been so easy. *Mr. Sullivan sounded as if he knew that people must spend thousands of dollars before they see any rewards.* Justin smiled to himself as he walked home. He was now more aware of the game that credit card companies played. He wondered to himself about how much money people lost on credit cards that have a much higher annual fee—all for the sake of getting a potential reward.

---

38 It is better to convert a credit card with the same credit card company than to cancel a credit card. If you cancel, you risk hurting your credit rating and credit score. Converting with the same company generally may allow you to keep your credit intact, and it may allow you to keep your accrued points. If the rewards points are not preserved with a conversion, redeem what you can, and *then* convert the old credit card to a new free rewards card.

Getting a Better Credit Card

Justin was on a roll. *I wonder if I can get a bigger rewards card for free.* He decided to return to www.creditcards.com, and there he found one that offered 50,000 sky miles, or two round-trip tickets. He applied for a credit card and was approved for a small credit limit. The card would arrive in about 10 days. Justin needed it by the end of the week in order to complete the assignment to automate his fixed payments. He elected to call the credit card company to ask if they could give him a temporary card with the same account number, explaining that he wanted to transfer his fixed payments to this one card.

The representative said that there was no such thing as a temporary credit card number. However, she said she could expedite the card so that it arrived sooner.

"That would be really nice," Justin responded. He gave his confirmation number from the credit card approval, and the representative said the card would arrive in two business days.

Recap—Start of Dreams

The next day Justin went on a run with Paul. Paul and Justin had been running together since they started their business.[39]

"Tell me again what the man did when you pointed out how much you had to spend before getting points," Paul requested.

"He was just kind of dumbfounded and didn't really have a rebuttal—kind of like he knew exactly that paid credit cards like the one that I used to use were a waste of money," Justin replied, reiterating the story of Mr. Sullivan and Justin's low-return paid credit card.

Paul laughed in disbelief. "Man, that is just crazy. You have even got me thinking of how to reduce my wasted money that I spend. You really lucked out with this class."

"I know. It really has been a gift from God. But get this... I checked at credit.com and I can get a rewards credit card that offers enough points for two round-trip plane tickets to most places in North America and either a rental car or one night at a mid-level hotel. The only catch

---

39 See Winning the *Money Game in College: Business,* by the author.

is that I have to spend $2,000 in two months. With tuition coming up next semester, that'll be easy–"

"Wait," interjected Paul, "credit cards are the worst way to pay for school because they have such high rates. Why would your professor tell you to use one of those?"

"I already have the cash for next semester, so I would pay it off in full before any interest accrued."

"So where are you going to go? Wait, let me guess… El Paso, Texas." Paul said with a smile. Justin frowned.

"Detroit?" Paul asked wryly.

"I was thinking of using all my points to take me to…"

"Machu Picchu," Paul and Justin said in unison.

"I knew that," Paul said with a smile. "You've been talking about it since we were in Ecuador. I just thought that it was kind of a dream, but now I can see that you have a plan, and I believe you will get there."

"Thanks," Justin smiled. "You should come with me. Let's do it next August."

"I would love to; it's just that Anna and I are getting close and you might be coming to my wedding at that time."

"Did you propose?" Justin asked curiously.

"Not yet, but perhaps soon," Paul said with a smile.

Later that day, Justin was trying to decide how, and if, he was going to contribute to a self-directed Roth IRA. Additionally, he had to investigate the Utah 529 Educational Savings Plan—all of that on top of automating his finances. Professor Christensen had made it clear that you did not have to *contribute* to a 401(k), Roth IRA, or 529 Savings Plan; you only had to investigate them and write a report on them.

Using Education Savings Plan

When he was done, Justin decided to go online and learn more about the Utah Educational Savings Plan (UESP). Justin went to *www.uesp.org* and found that they had an investment similar to life cycle funds, but these funds were *anticipated* educational funds or age-based funds, where you pick the date that you want your funds to be available. The plan had low fees, and the money could be used at any accredited educational institution. Additionally, since he was now working in Utah, he could claim a statewide tax credit of 5%, up to certain limits of earnings.

What caught Justin's attention were the age-based funds, the funds similar to the life cycle funds, or target date funds mentioned by Professor Christensen. He read over the handout and found that life cycle funds would automatically take care of diversification and allocation of money and cycle the money for different periods. Since he was young, he could be aggressive and grow his money by investing in stock-based mutual funds. When he was older, he'd want a mix of bonds and stock-based mutual funds. When Justin was finally ready to use his money someday, the handout said, he'd want it mostly in money market accounts and bond funds—these being the least risky.

Justin, at this point, was at a loss of what to do. *Should I put my money in a Roth IRA and not access it for years, or should I put it in an educational savings plan and get a low return?* He concluded that he needed to better define his goals and get more information. He decided to take a five-minute break, so between classes, he put up a sign saying 'Back in 5 min.'

Justin called the UESP contact number. He asked the representative for which expenses the plan could be used.

"The Utah Educational Savings Plan can be used for any accredited educational institution in the USA: tuition; book reimbursement for actual costs; room and board; and for lab or class fees," the phone receptionist said.

"Are there any special benefits for me if I work in Utah?" Justin asked.

"You can get a 5% state credit on your taxes, up to the set limit," the receptionist said.

"If I wanted to use the money in less than three years, what should I invest in to keep my money safe?" Justin asked.

"I cannot give financial or legal advice," the receptionist responded. "However, I can connect you with a plan-sponsored financial planner."

"That would be great," Justin said.

The receptionist put him through to the financial planner. Justin explained his dilemma, stating that he wanted the money to be available in less than three years.

"Keep in mind," said the financial planner, "that you get a 5% state income tax credit for working in Utah. That is like getting a 5% return on your money simply because you didn't spend it but saved it. To make things a little better for you, why don't you invest in…?" The financial planner gave Justin a plan that would allow his money to grow and told him which funds would give him the best return for such a short period of time while remaining as safe as possible.

"Remember," the financial advisor added, "the returns aren't guaranteed. They can go down, but that is a fairly safe plan for a one, two, and three-year outlook, and you can still get the tax credit on top of it. Even though the return will probably be less than 2%, this is still better than most CDs or money market accounts. Just be sure to use the money only for qualified expenses, and you'll be fine. The money won't be taxed when you take it out—including any growth—as long as you use it on qualified expenses."

Justin thanked the financial planner for his time.

Justin reviewed his goals he had made earlier: going to Machu Picchu, graduating without credit card or student loan debt, and purchasing a property before he graduated and came to a decision. *If I set a goal to purchase a property in three years or less, and continue to save for Machu Picchu, I'll get 5% credited from what I would have spent on state income tax, plus what I can get on my return from investing, and I can use the money for the most expensive parts of a college education—including housing,* Justin mused. *As long as I continue to save in my money market account, that is the route for me,* he concluded. *My goal of buying a property using a 529 savings plan sounds like a good one.* He went back to work and signed up for the UESP 529.[40]

As part of the savings plan, Justin decided to put in $1,000 to start. He linked the plan to his checking account. The money was withdrawn and the funds were processed. Justin then remembered that the last part of the assignment was to automate all of his finances. He thought

---

40 See *Winning the Money Game in College: Real Estate* to learn more.

about how Allison was able to automatically contribute to her 401(k) plan from her paycheck. He went back to the rules for his 529 ESP and looked for the info. Sure enough, he could contribute to his 529 plan directly from his paycheck in the same way that direct deposits were done at the bank.

I get paid twice per month, so if I just set up a contribution of $200 per paycheck to the savings plan and money from scholarships, I can have all the money I need to buy a property in less than 3 years or use the money for tuition. Justin logged into his e-mail and clicked the link that Kevin, his boss, had given him, which led him back to his employee portal. He added the newly formed account information for the UESP, to deposit $200 from each paycheck into the plan.

Justin was already seeing results from automating his financial matters. Honestly, he felt a little excited to just get everything done so that it didn't require a lot of maintenance and upkeep. Justin wanted to focus on school, and it was nice to know that his finances were being taken care of automatically.

Linking Credit Cards with Checking Accounts

True to its word, the company sent Justin's new rewards credit card to arrive in two days. Justin called in to confirm receiving the card and got it activated. He then asked to speak with a representative.

"Good morning, Mr. Murray," the representative said. "What can I do for you?"

"Well," said Justin, "I was wondering how I would link my new credit card to my checking account and set it up so the card will automatically pull money from my checking account each month and pay off the entire balance in full."

"That's a great question," the representative said. "You will need to have your account number and routing number and either provide them over the phone or log into your account online and do it there."

"I think that I'd like to complete it online," Justin said.

The representative told Justin how to link his checking account to the credit card and then confirm the linked accounts. The representative also told Justin how to set up the billing so that it would automatically pay each month, allowing Justin to pick the day he wanted the money to be pulled from his checking account.

When Justin had a moment to get online, he linked his checking account and credit card and then chose the tenth day of the month to pay off the credit card in full. He noticed a section called *E-mail Alerts*, and he set up both an alert to go to his e-mail and a text reminder to go to his cell phone so that he'd be sure to have deposited enough money in his account when that drafting occurred.

Automating Payments with Credit Cards and BillPay

On *this* credit card, Justin was only going to put his fixed expenses that allowed credit card payments with no additional fees. He'd use BillPay for other fixed expenses.

Justin decided to put everything he could onto automatic bill paying by using both the BillPay service and his rewards credit card to pay his fixed bills. He figured that since rent was due on the fifth of the month, he would pay every other fixed expense on that day as well.

Justin logged onto each account for his cell phone, auto insurance, and Internet Company, and copied his account numbers, address where to send his payments, and checked if they had the ability to pay by credit card. After finding the information, he copied the addresses for payment, along with other pertinent account information, such as the account number for each bill, into MS Excel, just for a quick reference since some of the websites would log him off. He already knew where to send his rent, and now he could pay all of his fixed expenses using BillPay or his rewards credit card.

Justin then went to each account and changed his billing information. His car insurance already allowed him to use his credit card directly, so he figured, *Well, why don't I make that payment due on the first, and have it automatically bill my credit card, then I can pay my credit card off on the fifth of the month—the same day rent is due, just to remind myself to pay all my bills on that day?* He went to the website for auto insurance and called a representative to change his billing date to the first of the month and have his credit card billed directly. The attendant was happy to oblige and make these changes. In passing, Justin mentioned the fact that he was a student at a university.

"Oh, you started school? That's wonderful!" remarked the agent. "Did you happen to know we offer a student discount on our car insurance?"

"No, I didn't," said Justin.

"Well, we do. All you have to do is maintain at least a 'B' average in your classes, and we will consider you to be a good student. At present, do you have that?"

Justin thought about his classes, and the grades he'd received. He was pretty sure he had well over a 'B' average, in fact closer to the 'A' range. He mentioned that to the attendant.

She said, "Great! Why don't we apply *this* discount to you as well?"

Justin was very grateful and thought, *Wow! This could come in handy.*

After setting up his auto insurance to draft on the first day of the month to the credit card he had chosen with a rewards plan, Justin then followed suit with his Internet provider and his cell phone.

After putting those bills on his credit card, and setting the credit card to be paid off in full each month, Justin decided to pay his rent by BillPay. He logged onto his checking account, searched, and arranged for a check to arrive by the first day of each month, even though it wasn't due until the fifth. He wanted to be cautious, in case there might ever be any major holidays to prevent the mail from being delivered exactly by the fifth.

Fluctuating Expenses—Get a Pre-Paid Debit Card

Justin figured that he would spend no more than $265 per month on fluctuating expenses: $150 for food, $80 for gasoline, and $35 for the rest. If he had any money left over from his food or gasoline allotments, he could spend that, but no more. He then added together the fluctuating expenses, his tithing, and his fixed expenses, and arranged to have that total amount transferred from his money market account to his checking account by the first of each month. Justin realized that since he set up the BillPay check to arrive by the second of each month, he needed to have money to pay rent transferred to his checking account to be withdrawn by the 25th of each month. This counted as a separate withdrawal from his money market account; Justin still had 4 withdrawals left. This meant that the money from his money market account would automatically transfer into his checking account where it would then be used to pay off his credit card and BillPay fixed expenses; the rest was his to spend as he pleased.

Justin was relieved that he no longer needed to worry about being late for his bill payments; they were all taken care of automatically. He wrote his one-page paper, describing what he had done to automate his financial life. In the paper, he also mentioned that he was earning about 1% interest from a money market account, saving about 2% from purchases he would have made anyway, and saving 5% by contributing to his 529 savings plan by not being taxed on state income tax (saving however much that grew), and preventing spending too much by using a prepaid-debit card—all done automatically. He was now free to spend $265 in the manner he deemed best—in addition to saving for his dreams of going to Machu Picchu, buying a property, and providing for future goals and ambitions in his 529 Savings Plan and his money market account. Life just got better financially, that's for sure.

Justin submitted his paper on the class website and then went looking for a scholarship to which he could submit his essay. He went to *www.fastweb.com* and found a scholarship easily. *More free money, here I come!*

Chapter 11: Principles and Suggestions

1. Automate your paycheck going to a money market account using direct deposit.

   a. Ensure that you follow the instructions for listing dependents on your W-2, W-4, and other tax forms.

2. Pay all of your fixed expenses on a designated rewards credit card and BillPay.

   a. Pay your credit card off in full each month by linking your credit card and checking account.

   b. Don't carry this card with you. Keep it separate from your regular purchases.

3. Pay your fluctuating expenses on a prepaid-debit card.

4. Link your money market account, checking account, and credit cards so that your paycheck goes into the money market, then to the checking account, then to pay your bills and credit cards.

5. Ask work about tuition reimbursement, scholarships, and 401(k) plans. Apply as directed.

6. Establish a Utah 529 Education Savings Plan. Contribute monthly, and use this to save up for tuition, books, and housing while getting a tax break as you save.

7. Each month withdraw the amount you need for fluctuating expenses and automatically have this deposited to your prepaid-debit card.

Chapter 11: Warnings and Avoidance

1. Don't pay for a rewards credit card unless you really get high rewards. It makes no sense to spend $20 per year at 1% return; you need to spend $2,000 before you even make a profit. There are lots of free rewards credit cards.

2. Banks will charge you if you use a debit or credit card and go over your balance; this is why it is recommended to use a pre-paid debit card to avoid bank fees.

3. You may need to transfer some expenses (like rent) earlier from your money market account into your checking account at an earlier date than what you pay for your credit cards and other bills. Try to add up the totals you need and then transfer them to your checking account in a grouped amount (i.e. $20 for laundry, $100 for food, $40 for cell phone = $180; withdraw $180 one time instead of 3 withdrawals).

Even though things happen automatically, it is still a good idea to review every account at least monthly.

Chapter 12: Consequences

Justin was running low on groceries; it was time to go to the store. After work, he stopped by his apartment to grab some grocery store ads. He'd started applying Professor Christensen's tip of price matching[41]—especially on produce. It cut his food bill down by a third. He still hadn't managed to price match everything—which he hoped, but it sure made for a better shopping trip when he saved some money.

At the checkout isle, he saw his cousin Dave. Dave was buying some snacks from the checkout aisle racks. "Hey, Justin! How's the college life treating you?"

"Pretty good," Justin said. "I started dating this girl I met in one of my classes."

"Is she cute?" Dave asked.

"Oh, yeah," Justin said for emphasis.

"Well, you should invite her over to our house for dinner. We'd love to meet her."

They talked for a few more minutes. Justin decided it would be fun to see Dave and Susan again, so they decided on Saturday. They set up the time and agreed to meet up.

Saturday came and Justin drove Allison over to meet his cousin and his family. While they were eating, Dave turned to Allison and asked "Justin told me that you two met in a class… which class was it?"

"We met in a personal finance class taught by a visiting professor," Allison explained.

---

41 Go to *www.CollegeCashChampion.com* to get this handout.

"Wow. No offense—sounds kind of boring. I thought you might have said tennis or ballroom dance or something like that," Dave said with a smile.

Allison laughed, "Well, I thought the class would be boring too, but it's been really helpful. We've been learning about real estate, managing finances, and something I really liked was something called a *Bubblegum-Diamond-Thief*," Allison said.

"What's a bubblegum diamond thief?" Susan asked.

"A Bubblegum-Diamond-Thief is what robs you of your money. You know, the type of stuff that is just quick purchases—maybe two dollars here or 75 cents each day. Well, those types of quick purchases prevent you from having what you really want, and at the end of the month you wonder where all your money went." Allison's enthusiasm showed clearly.

"No kidding," said Dave said with a smile. "What did your professor say to do to stop this thief?"

"He taught us to set a big goal that's really important to us, and then determine what we are willing to sacrifice to achieve it," Allison began.

Justin noticed Susan's lower lip was starting to tremble.

"Sacrifice doesn't mean that we stop having fun," Allison continued, "It just means we do things differently—like waiting to borrow or rent a movie instead of going to see the movie in theaters, or making lunch instead of buying fast food, and finding expenses we don't need, like paying interest on credit cards."

"Did your professor say to get rid of credit cards altogether?" Dave asked.

"Well, no, he actually told us to get a credit card that offers good rewards, not one of those cards that come in the mail. He also said we should pay off our bills in full and on time, but do it automatically, so you don't have to worry about it, and then get a prepaid-debit card to use for day-to-day purchases. That way you never get a late notice, and you won't overspend your money or get hit with an overcharge. The money comes into your savings account, and then some goes to your goals, future bills, fixed expenses, and your prepaid-debit card. It has really saved me a lot of worry about money…"

Compound Bad Decisions—What Debt REALLY Means

With the mention of worry about money, Susan couldn't hold it in any longer and the tears started flowing as she cried.

"Did I say something to offend you?" Allison asked, worried she had said something impolite.

"All we ever do is worry about money," Susan sobbed. Dave put his hand on her shoulder.

"It'll be alright, honey," Dave said. "We'll make it work."

"No we won't! You are always working, and we never seem to catch up," Susan exclaimed through her tears.

"We didn't mean to upset you," Justin said with compassion; he remembered seeing the overdue notice when he was here.

"It's not your fault, it's ours," Susan said.

"Honey," Dave began.

"No, they should know what it's like on the other side—so they never make the same mistakes we made," Susan retorted, sounding resolute through her tears. Without waiting she continued.

"We both got credit cards when we were in college. I got a stupid water bottle that I lost within a few weeks, for getting a credit card. It seemed so exciting while I was on campus to get that card. I would go to restaurants with my friends, buy a new outfit, and buy junk that I can't even remember now. I thought that 'I'd pay it off later,' and boy have we paid for it later."

"Dave had about the same problems with money as I did. When we were engaged, we just thought that once we graduated we'd get a better job and pay off all our debts, credit cards, and student loans… but it didn't happen that way." Susan took a breath between her sobs.

"We found we could spend more because we were earning more. We bought a bigger house than we needed. We bought a new car because it was just $788 per month. We never realized we'd end up paying over $35,000 for a car that was worth $23,000. But pretty soon, it became hard to keep up with it all. Do you know what it's like having $43,000 in credit card debt, $11,000 left on a car payment, student loans, and a mortgage? It's horrible and depressing; our paycheck is gone by mid-month. The interest alone... it should be criminal to charge anything over 20 percent."

"Honey, I can just put more hours into my job. Could we talk about this later, I mean it's really not that bad," Dave said, noticeably embarrassed.

"Put more hours, into your job?! You're already working 60 hours a week now. We don't have money and you're gone so much, and we can't afford to even consider having a baby because we can't control our expenses. It *is* that bad. I looked at the credit card today and our stacks of bills. When you go to the store, you come home with junk food and you tell me 'It's no big deal.' We have to pay for things over and over because we never learned to manage money. We keep paying for it later and later. The more we do that, the harder it becomes... and in the end all we have is a bunch of worthless junk."

Susan just sobbed and sobbed. There was a heavy uneasiness in the room. "As you can tell, we have been kind of struggling," Dave said remorsefully.

"Everyone makes mistakes," Justin said. "I could drop off a copy of the handout our professor gave us called *Setting Yourself Up to Win,* but what you might need is to ultimately find out how you can save money."

"A government-sponsored debt counselor might be able to help." Allison said.

Dave nodded absently. Most of his attention was on comforting his wife.

Justin turned to Allison and said, "We should go."

Allison nodded.

"Dave, you and Susan can keep the salad and the potatoes," Justin said, wanting to help, but it clearly only made Dave feel worse to receive free food from a college student.

Dave gave a half-smile and nodded.

"I'll drop that handout by later," Justin quickly added.

Justin and Allison said their goodbyes and left. When in the car, there was still a heavy feeling. Dave and Susan's dilemma was on both of their minds. Allison was the first to break the silence:

"Sorry about your cousin and his wife," Allison said carefully.

"Me too," Justin replied. "I never realized that they were hurting so much because of money. All I can say is that I understand why Professor Christensen was so adamant about staying out of debt. It really does crush you."

"I never want to get into debt for things that don't increase in value," Allison said. "I'm so glad that Professor Christensen warned us about avoiding debt and watching our Bubblegum-Diamond-Thief."

Chapter 12: Principles and Suggestions

1. Match ads where you can at stores. You can save a lot of money.

2. Teach others about the concepts you learn. Don't plagiarize, but do teach the concepts you learn to others to help them.

3. Learn to pay for things you can afford; if you wait to pay till later, later does come, but usually with a higher price tag.

Chapter 12: Warnings and Avoidance

1. You can avoid the emotional and financial consequences of debt by watching your Bubblegum-Diamond-Thief and living within your means.

2. Stay away from debt consolidation companies. These types of companies tend to be dishonest.

3. Being in debt really takes the life out of you. Avoid being in debt for things that depreciate. Pay off your bills in full.

Chapter 13: Staying Out of Financial Trouble

During the next class, Professor Christensen said that he wanted to talk about something very important. "Let's talk about expenses."

The True Cost of Debt

"I hope that, with all the time I've spent teaching you about applying for scholarships, you've minimized your expenses; but if not, we're going to talk about that right now. I know that we covered some of this before, but I think it's important to bring it up again. One financial blogger who accrued massive amounts of credit card debt bemoaned that she'd spent money on things she didn't need, and then didn't have money when she actually did need it. Another blogger said that the time that was wasted prevented her from taking other opportunities because of the debt that was accumulated.[42] Doesn't that make you a little sick to hear?

"First and foremost, establish some type of budgeting or accounting system. You need to pay off your credit card in full—every month. If you make large purchases (paying for tuition, for example), rather than just putting it on the credit card and working to pay off the credit card, do it in reverse. Have enough cash in your account to pay off the entire balance, and then try to find a good rewards card and get some money back. But no matter what else, pay off your credit card debt in full every month. This will allow you to avoid late charges, interest, and penalties, and it will allow you to improve your credit. I can't stress this enough. There are so many Americans who are maxing

---

42 'Emma'. "Mistakes Made with Money." CNN.com Blogs. Accessed April 19, 2014. http://cnnstudent-news.blogs.cnn.com/2010/04/22/mistakes-made-with-money/.

out their credit cards, and it's just, figuratively speaking, eating them alive."

Professor Christensen asked if anyone had the handout called "Setting Yourself Up to Win." Tyler replied that he did. Professor Christensen asked Tyler to turn to the section entitled *'final thoughts.'* Tyler read:

Debt is slavery. Debt is a thief. Debt steals our todays with worry and concern and robs our hope for tomorrows. People spend money that they haven't yet earned, on the assumption that they will pay out their tomorrows by purchasing on credit; however, they pay for it over and over again. Debt is a dragon that eats people's lives. People are working over and over again for the same items...

After Tyler read the quote, Professor Christensen asked: "Do you think that this is true about debt? Why or why not?" Justin knew this wasn't the setting, but he couldn't help thinking of Dave and Susan and what had happened at their house—when Susan cried and cried over their finances. *Debt really is a dragon that eats people,* Justin thought to himself. Other students started answering the professor's question.

"Well, if you don't have a car to go to work, wouldn't getting a car help people make more money? I mean, wouldn't that be good debt?" Ashley inquired.

"I work off campus," Tyler responded; "even with my job I have to pay gas and insurance for my car—plus the car payment. I thought I needed a car, but it's costing me money. I have my job, and I have some freedom, but I didn't realize what the freedom was costing me. I started thinking after Professor Christensen's lesson on managing expenses and the handout *Setting Yourself Up to Win*, that I was spending about half of my paycheck just to have the car. I wish I'd gotten a closer job so I didn't need to commute, or at least not bought my car on an auto loan. Now I'm stuck paying for it for the next three years. I am a slave to my car, instead of having complete freedom."

"Wait, *dude*–" Malcolm interjected, "are you serious?! How do you ever expect to get a date if you can't even show the ladies that you can afford to take care of yourself?"

"I hadn't thought of that," Tyler said.

"Well, some of us 'ladies'," Allison said, giving a slight glare at Malcolm, "care more about who you are as a person, than your car. Let me put it this way: what if your 'lady' marries you for your nice car; when will it stop? Getting a more expensive house than you can afford? Buying a luxury diamond and 18 karat gold necklace? Taking expensive vacations? Paying for her expensive designer wardrobe? If you start your relationship based on high material expectations, you will constantly have to meet and exceed this high standard. My dad taught me to look more at the person than the material things. He says that a lack of finances causes divorce, and I should never be the person that marries or dates someone just for his money. I would much rather marry a guy who manages his money well and has no debt, than a guy who spends too much to buy presents he can't afford and is constantly racking up the bills."

"Well," Malcolm retorted sarcastically, "aren't you just Miss-Goodie-Two-Shoes?"

"Malcolm," Professor Christensen immediately spoke up, "you owe Allison an apology. Remember the rules of this class: we are to respect each other and maintain a positive attitude. Allison, you need to apologize as well... your point was well taken, but a little rude."

Malcolm apologized, though he sounded a little sullen. Allison was more sincere.

Justin made silent note of Allison's response about money. He decided to ask a question. "Excuse me, Professor. From what I remember of your handout, you said that we should only go into debt to acquire assets that appreciate. I understand that real estate appreciates, but why did you tell us to avoid student loans?"

"Excellent question," Professor Christensen said. "Student loans may be helpful, but first consider these points:

1. You'll be paying interest and school will cost you more.

2. There are very few things that you can actually do to get rid of your student loans. Even if you were to declare bankruptcy, your student loans would still be there.

3. It may be an unnecessary expense, as there are grants, scholarships, tuition reimbursement, and jobs that may help you completely cover your college costs.

4. If the economy is bad when you graduate, you may not have access to money to pay these debts. The very best you can do is delay payments, but that only increases the interest that you pay.

"Just because student loans are easy to get into does not mean they are the best thing for you. To some degree, student loans are like credit cards; fairly easy to obtain, but they come with a hefty price tag with interest and penalties."

The Negatives of Credit Cards

"Credit cards can hurt you. Does anyone want to share some negative things that they have seen about credit cards?" Professor Christensen asked.

"My dad and mom bought things on credit cards," Ashley stated. "They eventually had to declare bankruptcy because they couldn't keep up with the interest and fees."

"My cousin," Allison added, "was going to college and got a credit card that was mailed to him. The card had a 29% interest rate and the ironic thing was that there was only a two day grace period. The card advertised that it was a great starter card, but my cousin could barely make a payment on time because of how the card payment cycles behaved."

"My problem with credit cards is that my card is not universally accepted at all stores," Malcolm added.

"Do you see the problems here?" Professor Christensen asked. "Credit cards are easy to obtain and merchants make it easy for you to use them in most cases. People got into trouble in one of two ways: one, they got the wrong type of card that has fees, a small grace period, high interest rates, or lack of flexibility in some other way; or two, they didn't pay their credit cards off in full every month—they borrowed too much from the future. Simply by looking at the terms and conditions of a card, getting free rewards cards, having enough money in the bank, and paying your card off in full each month, you can avoid the major pitfalls of credit cards.

"I recommend you get a prepaid-debit card, and predetermine what you will spend your money on, and then only carry this prepaid-debit or prepaid credit card to avoid overspending. It doesn't matter whether you are an individual, a small business, or corporation; the only time that you should ever go into debt is when the purchase will appreciate or return a greater value to you. If you don't pay your bills on time you get a fee, when you exceed your balance you get a fee, when you get cash advances, you generally get a fee. Instead, decide what you really want and then create a plan to get it."

The Benefits of Using a Good Credit Card

"What good is having a credit card compared to a debit card or just paying cash?" Allison asked.

"In addition to building credit and getting rewards," Professor Christensen replied, "from the American Express website[43], here are some of the benefits:

- Free rental car insurance.
- Free extra year of manufacturer's warranty on most purchases.
- Free return coverage for 90 days to return unwanted items purchased.
- Free travel accidental insurance.
- Free entertainment guides and services to get concert tickets and other entertainment services (must pay for entertainment purchased).

Building Credit

"Now, let's talk about building credit. Here's a simple way you can build credit—just an idea. Go to a bank and deposit $500 (or an amount that works for you) into an account. Take out a loan, for about

43 American Express. "Credit Cards & Charge Cards." Accessed April 19, 2014. https://www304.americanexpress.com/credit-card?inav=footer_cards_personal.

90% of what you put in (in this case, $450), the loan absolutely must not have a pre-payment penalty. Offer the $500 as collateral. Set up an automatic payment with the bank to pay back the amount of the loan over at least six months. The bank will automatically pay the loan so you will not need to worry about it. You need six months to be able to establish good credit.

"What this will do is record a positive payment history with a bank on your credit profile. The financial institution automatically pays from your deposit account, whether it's checking or savings, or in some cases, a money market account, paying off your loan automatically. What that'll do is allow them to pay it off over the course of the loan. Make sure there's no prepayment penalty. That way, if ever you want to end the loan early, you may do so. This will increase your credit by having an established history of good financial payment with an installment loan."

(To get a free report on how to improve credit, and other bonuses, go to *www.CollegeCashChampion.com* and click on refer a friend.)

The bell rang. Professor Christensen dismissed the class.

Chapter 13: Principles and Suggestions

1.	Find ways to stay out of debt: Pay for school using scholarships, grants, and jobs that offer tuition reimbursement.

2.	Establish relationships on interaction not material possessions.

3.	Get a rewards credit cards that includes the following:

	a.	Grace period of at least 20 days (i.e., the time that you have to pay your bill after each billing cycle).

	b.	A reward of at least 1% of your total purchase points.

	c.	Free fraud protection for any charge not made or authorized by you.

	d.	Free rewards program—unless you can get a really good benefit to be used by you immediately, such as a trip or points that far exceed the cost of the card.

    i.   Keep in mind the break-even equation when you calculate your rewards; spending $19 per year for a 1% rewards card is not worth it.

4. Review the section on benefits of using a credit card.

5. An idea to build credit: take $500 and go to one lending institution, take 90% and go to another bank, take 90% of that go to a third lending institution. Each time setup automatic payments to pay off the amounts.

Chapter 13: Warnings and Avoidance

1. Credit card companies target students; avoid credit card offers that come in the mail or can be found at a booth on campus. These cards have some of the fewest advantages, highest penalties, and highest interest rates."

2. Avoid credit card debt by selecting the right card at the start, and pay your credit card off in full every month.

    a.   Get a prepaid-debit card to help control spending.

3. Check with your accountant for which type of account is right for you: IRA, 401(k), or 529 Savings account.

4. NEVER get into a relationship based on money—whether you are the one paying or the one receiving. Don't use money or other possessions to be the primary way that you bring someone into your life. Let that happen by your personality and interactions.

Chapter 14: Last Hoorah

After class, Justin went up to Professor Christensen and asked about Dave and Susan's predicament—without revealing confidential information, to find out if there was anything that Professor Christensen could suggest they do. After hearing a few details, Professor Christensen replied:

"One of the things that they can do is call their credit card companies and explain their circumstances," Professor Christensen said. "Specifically ask if their credit card companies have a debt management program—one where they will lock the credit card from being used for 12 to 18 months *and* during the credit card freeze if they can have 0% (or close to 0%) interest on the balance. Often, people with debt try to hide their problems; if they can just explain their situation, they *may* be able to have their credit card companies work with them."

"Next, they need to take control of their spending. You should tell them about the pre-paid debit card idea and channeling their money. This still works even for married people not in school. Specifically, they need to learn about their *Bubblegum-Diamond-Thieves* and stop them. They need to make a plan to take their extra money and put it towards their debt. I am also guessing that they are not saving; they should try to put some money towards a 401(k) plan or other retirement account. I know that it is really hard for people to save when they are in debt, but it is the habit and principle that they need to establish—while getting whatever free money they can from their employer. Additionally, as long as they can establish a pattern of savings, if they cannot pay their debts and must declare bankruptcy, generally speaking the bankruptcy courts will not touch retirement accounts—assuming that there is an established pattern of contribution (you can't just stick whatever money you have in a retirement account and then soon thereafter, declare bankruptcy). I'd recommend that they also read David Bach's book *Debt Free for Life*."

"That should get them started," Professor Christensen said. "Getting out of debt is hard, but worth it. Just make sure that they are also creating ways to grow their money."

"Thank you professor," Justin said. "I think that will help them a lot."

"Sure thing," Professor Christensen said right before he and Justin parted.

Crunch Time—Focusing on Finances

The semester was coming to a close. Justin's business was doing well and he had hopes of purchasing a property. After looking at several properties, Justin had chosen to get one under contract. However, right after getting it under contract, Justin's business experienced an unexpected loss—this loss was huge and took his company's profits down to about zero. (To read more about this, please read *Winning the Money Game in College: Business*.)

"How am I going to pay for my property now?" Justin was bemoaning to Allison. "I mean, it's just not fair."

"Justin," Allison said in a sympathetic tone, "I'm sorry about this loss. I know it hurts and it is not fair. Do you remember the first day of class and Professor Christensen asked if the students who left class were victims or victors?"

"Yes," Justin responded, "that was when I first started to get to know you. You said something about them choosing their attitude."

"Look, at one point in my parents' married lives, my dad was working as a lower level manager of a company. He made an okay living, but he was miserable. One day, the company needed to downsize and he was laid off with a severance package. At first my dad was panic stricken having me and my brothers and sisters to provide for. My mom simply kissed him and told him, 'Now the world gets to see the real man that I married; but more importantly, my husband gets to see the man who he really is. Sweetheart, let's take the money from the severance and have you choose what it is that you really want to do.

I love you and I will support your decision, but, I want you to choose what you really want to do.'"

"My dad kissed my mom, took the message, and decided that he liked people and had a fascination with helping people look nice; he thought about it and decided he wanted to be a barber. He went to school, and got to do what he loved. He learned to manage his money, and mom commented that he was never happier. My dad said once upon reflection, 'I am so glad that I was laid off; it allowed me to do what I really love.' Justin, you can either choose to be a victim of your circumstances or you can do something about it—either way, I believe in you and love you."

Justin smiled and said, "That was a great story, and I think you are right: I need to remain positive. But I think you left something out of the story."

"What's that?" Allison asked.

"This," Justin said as he embraced then kissed Allison. The kiss was the type of kiss that fills the two people with butterflies and excitement all at the same time.

"Oh, I see," said Allison with a smile.

"Thank you so much," Justin said to emphasize Allison's comment. "Thanks for helping me to shift my perspective."

"Sure, no problem," Allison responded.

"What do you think that I should do about the property?" Justin asked, returning to the topic at hand.

"Is it a good deal?" Allison asked.

"Yeah," replied Justin.

"Does it meet the credentials Professor Christensen suggested?"

"I would only consider it if it did."

"Then it is worth fighting for," Allison replied. "You've got to be willing to do some things differently."

"Yeah, you're right. But what do I do?" Justin asked.

"Fall break is coming up," Allison reminded Justin, "I will be away. Why don't you spend the bulk of it applying to scholarships? I'll bet you could apply to 20-25 of them—especially using your system. You just need to know the money is coming; you can then divert some of your money towards this property."

"That's a good idea," Justin replied. "But it has got to be more. I hate to say it, but I think it is time to sell my car and perhaps for a short term, cut my expenses drastically."

"Those would definitely help. It sounds like you have the beginnings of a plan," Allison commented. "Between your business, scholarships, and cutting expenses you just might make it. How much time do you have?"

"Two and a half weeks."

"Justin, when you started this semester, from what you have told me, you couldn't even pay for tuition, but now you are paying for school, running a business, and buying a property," Allison said again shifting Justin's thinking.

"Thanks for helping create a plan."

"Sure, you may want to speak with Professor Christensen and get some ideas," Allison replied.

Honing In—What Can Happen When Focused

Justin emailed Professor Christensen about his dilemma. Professor Christensen thought that his plan of focusing on scholarships and businesses would be a good idea.

While Allison is gone, why don't I apply to at least 15 scholarships in one week and do some promotional deals with our business? This way I can at least say I did everything I could. But, first, I am going to put an ad up to sell my car.

Applying to so many scholarships seemed monotonous. It seemed like every application was the same: "Name," "Major," "GPA," "Address," and all the other similar fields. Justin felt compelled to give it his all. *I am so glad that I established this system before I needed to apply to so many scholarships so quickly.* Justin didn't know if he would make it, but figured that even if he got one additional $1,000 scholarship, he would be getting $40 to $60 per hour—which wasn't bad. Justin really wanted to get this property though. It was that important to him, not just because of the deal, but he wanted to see what he could accomplish if he pushed himself.

Justin also focused on his business. It was picking up — especially, getting close to the Christmas season. Allison returned from fall break. Several people had called about Justin's car, but no real takers. A student named Fred called and asked if he could see it. Justin replied that he could.

"I'll take it," Fred said after taking a test drive. "If you'll stop by this bank ATM, I will get cash to pay you."

"Don't you want to go inside the bank—it's just down the street?" Justin asked. "You can avoid the ATM fee."

"Don't worry about it," Fred said. "The fees are only about two dollars."

Justin knew that he couldn't tell Fred how to spend his money, but Justin couldn't help thinking *Warning, Bubblegum-Diamond-Thief in Progress! Warning, Bubblegum-Diamond-Thief.*

After Fred paid, Justin filled out the paperwork to transfer title. Justin felt relieved. He didn't have to pay insurance, gas, or pay for repairs and registration. Justin had four days left before he had to either have the cash, or forfeit his property.

After speaking with his business partners, they decided to enter a student business competition. The contest was put on by professionals in the community. "It can't hurt us to apply," Justin had told his business partners.

"Yeah, I guess not," Paul said, in a tone that conveyed 'if you think so.'

Justin didn't know if they would win, but at least entering gave them free promotional exposure. Justin couldn't help but remember Mr. Wheatley's analogy of waiting standby for an airplane: we may get it if we apply, but if we don't at least apply, we definitely won't, even if there was an award that would have worked.

Between business, scholarships, and homework, Justin was glad that it was fall break, because most of his time was consumed. However, Justin did take the time to play a few games of tennis with Paul— the tennis helped to de-stress.

Chapter 14: Principles and Suggestions

1. Surround yourself with people who will lift you up.

2. Define your fears and make a plan to overcome.

3. When it matters to you, be willing to take risks. Justin wasn't risking too much because he was aware of his pull out date with his real estate.

Chapter 14: Warnings and Avoidance

1. Don't take just risks for the sake of taking risks. Instead take calculated risks—know what is at stake and how you prevent loss. Justin wanted to buy a property, but knew his pull-out date and he was only risking time and effort.

2. ep your worries and concerns in check. Often we feel overwhelmed by the "unknown." Define your fears and create a plan to overcome obstacles.

Chapter 15: Semester's End

Justin had spent most of his fall break applying to scholarships; he was able to apply to 17 scholarships—but he still didn't know if he would make it. Justin had received his paycheck on Friday. He wondered if he should pay his tithing now, or wait till after he bought his property. Justin decided to pay his tithing. *God is the best business partner I could ask for. Even if I don't get this property, He has already given me so much—including being in Professor Christensen's class.* Justin paid 10% of his earnings.

Justin had until Thursday to decide on the property. "I don't know if I am going to make it," Justin told Allison.

"That's okay, it is not the end of the world, but at least you can have no regrets knowing that you did your best."

"Yeah, you're right," Justin replied.

What happened over the next four days was actually really remarkable. Justin's business completed several contracts and Justin's share was part of what he needed. That same time Justin's business and teammates qualified for the final selection of contestants in the business contest—which automatically guaranteed them $1,000–$200 of which would be Justin's share. Justin was awarded a $4,000 scholarship and still had other scholarships that were pending. The scholarship came from one for which Justin had applied before fall break, but free money really was never something to be complained about. Additionally, Justin was given a cash gift from his grandpa. Justin was really overwhelmed. He had his money, and not just what he needed for the property, but also enough to pay for two semesters of college.

"I really don't believe it," Justin said to Allison. "I mean, two weeks ago I felt like I did when I started this semester—alone and cash-strapped, but everything really came together."

"You were so blessed, Justin," Allison replied. "It really was remarkable to see you accomplish all that you did."

"I don't think that I could have done it without you. You really encouraged me when I needed it. Thank you *so* much."

"Sure thing! You'd have done the same thing for me."

Justin and Allison continued their walk around Steed Park. "You seem pensive. What are you thinking about?" Allison asked Justin.

"Oh, I was just thinking about the class and all that we have learned."

"I know what you mean," Allison replied.

Truthfully, Justin had been thinking about an idea that came to him, but he replied "I am going to miss this class—and seeing you three times a week."

"What!?" Allison said with a smile. "I'm sure we could arrange to see each other three times per week."

Justin smiled. "Yeah, I think we could arrange that."

Gaining a Dream—Involving Others in Your Goal

After his date with Allison, Justin called Paul, "Hey, would you like to take a trip with me?"

"Where to? When?" Paul responded.

"How about going to Machu Picchu for spring break?"

"What?! Are you serious? I don't want to leave Anna."

"I never said we wouldn't bring her along—and for that matter, I want to bring Allison," Justin responded. "We'll stay in a place for us, and the girls will stay in a place for them so that everything stays Kosher."

"Great! How am I supposed to pay for two tickets?"

"You have the money for next semester's tuition right?"

"Yeah, but if you think I am going to use that money to go to Machu Picchu, you are crazy," Paul responded.

Justin reminded Paul about the rewards credit card that he had and the upfront bonus of two round-trip tickets. Justin also explained about getting the state tax credit by first putting the money into a 529 savings plan.

"You've already got the money. The credit card requires that we spend $2,000 within 100 days of opening the account. Guess what costs more than $2,000?"

"Tuition," Paul said, realizing where Justin was going with this idea. "I like it. I'm so doing that for spring break! Where do I get one of those credit cards?"

Justin gave the specifics on the credit card. "We can work out the rest of the details of the trip as we present the idea to the girls. I don't want to go there alone, so who better to bring than my best friend and girlfriend? I don't think it would be a good idea to invite Allison without Anna being there."

"Yeah, I know what you mean," Paul responded. "But this idea sounds awesome; I'm in as long as the girls are."

"Me, too," Justin replied.

Paul and Justin continued making plans—all the while, becoming more and more excited. After about 20 minutes, both of them agreed on their plan.

On the last week of class, Professor Christensen told the class, "Well, we have two things left. One is going to be a final project; it's a surprise. The other is an invitation to come to an assembly the university is putting on, on the 14th of December. The assembly will not be part of your grade and not required for this class, but you are welcome to come." Professor Christensen said the final project would be e-mailed to them later that day.

Calculating Net Worth

At work, Justin checked his e-mail and downloaded the attachments containing the final project instructions. They were as follows:

Get a clean, white sheet of paper and on it draw a line down the center, making two columns. The left column is for future semesters, if everything continues as is. The right column is for this present semester.

In the right column, write down the number of scholarships you applied to this semester and the approximate amount of money you made from scholarships this semester; make a subtotal. Then write down, in the same column, the money you gained from the businesses you started—this is a *personal* gain. Make a subtotal in the right column. Write down another subtotal if you made any money from real estate. Now write down your present expenses for this semester (rent, car payments, etc.), also in the right column. Subtotal both.

In left column, write down any *continued* scholarship monies that are scheduled to come. Then write down your future expenses if things continue as they are at this point. Subtotal them both.

In the right column list the major profitable items you have (i.e., car, cash) and their approximate values. Also list any expenses that you have (i.e., student loans, credit card debt, etc.)

Finally, subtract the expenses from the income in each column. Now you know what you get to keep both now and in the future if things continue as they are now. <u>Financially, 'at the end of the day,' it's what you *keep*, not what you earn, that counts.</u> This is the equivalent of totaling up your net worth. If you were to sell everything you have, at present market value, and subtract any debts or any expenses, *that's* your net worth. I hope that your net worth, now, is in the tens-of-thousands-of-dollars range.

Calculating Contribution Worth

Now turn the paper over. This side will have no columns. We're going to describe the contributions you have made. Write down the amount of service that you've done, in hours per month, and what you did. Total up these hours. Write down the amount and percentage of money you have contributed to charitable causes. Write down the number of people with whom that you have networked during your time here. Write down the books that you have read. Write down the classes that you've taken, both through the university and privately. Write down how you've done your part at your jobs. Write down any times that you've offered a smile to someone who was down. Write down the times that you told family and friends that you love them. Write down time that you've given for anyone that you've mentored. Write down the amount of time that you have given attention to God, for example, reading sacred writings, praying, attending services, etc.

<u>When it comes to making contributions and making a difference, 'at the end of the day,' it's what you give *away* that matters.</u> The more that you give of yourself, the more that you will have. The more love that you give away, the more that you will receive. The more that you teach others, the more that you learn for yourself. There are two things that matter when it comes to having a life of meaning. One is having the freedom you desire—part of which is control over your finances. Two and more importantly, is being contribution-minded. When you contribute, your life means something more than just sitting in front of the TV each day.

Complete both parts of the assignment. You need to email it to me by December 13th in order to receive credit.

Justin's Net Worth—Example of What Could Happen

Okay, let's see, Justin thought to himself. *I applied to 53 scholarships—thanks to my blitz during fall break. I earned 7 scholarships. Now what were the amounts? First, a scholarship for full tuition for 4 years, then a $2,000 scholarship… and finally the $4,000 scholarship I just received. Don't forget my Pell Grant and small scholarships from my dad's work. Now what's the total?*

Justin pulled out a calculator and after punching in the numbers almost dropped it. *Over $18,000 came to me in scholarships this semester?! I want to see it.* Justin then logged into his bank account with Ally, and couldn't believe it. He saw with his own eyes the money from his recent scholarships and business successes. The money was deposited automatically over the past week, so Justin wasn't fully aware of the total. He had over $15,000 in his high yield account; Justin had originally planned on using the few thousand he had for next semester's tuition. *Now thanks to the money I saved, and grandpa's gift in my 529 savings plan, I have enough for tuition in that account.* Justin was stunned. *That money in my account is after paying rent and food.* Justin added up all his money in his checking and 529 accounts; he was amazed at the total.

What about my expenses? Let's see, I'm paying rent right now, but I won't be soon, thanks to my property. I pay my cell phone. I don't have to pay gas or insurance now that I sold my car. I am left with food, fun, and my goals; tuition is already covered for next semester. He wrote everything down, and found his net worth was about $20,000.

Now on to the contribution phase of the assignment, Justin thought. *Let's see, I went singing, I went to the old folks home with Allison, I tried to be positive most of the time, I did my job well, I became better friends with Paul, I am dating a wonderful girl, I helped Dave and Susan, I attended church service…. Oh, wow! I had no idea I had such an impact, but more importantly, look at how I have benefitted. Sure, I helped others, but as I was helping them, they were helping me to be happier.* Justin continued to list things he had done to serve others. He completed the assignment, and then combined it with his net worth for grading. He sat for a while and thought about how many great things were happening in his life.

Assembly Surprises

On the 14th of December, the day after he had submitted his final report to Professor Christensen via e-mail, Allison and Justin walked, hand-in-hand, to the assembly that evening.

"What did you think of our last assignment?" Justin asked Allison.

"I thought it was amazing; I had no idea I had done so well," Allison responded. "I mean, when I added up my net worth I was shocked to see how much I had earned between business, scholarships, and soon-to-be real estate."

"I agree," Justin said. "What surprised me even more was how I had grown with my relationships and by giving service to others. I just took that stuff for granted, but when I saw my own report, I was amazed at how blessed I really am."

"We really owe Professor Christensen a lot," Allison said. "Without him, we wouldn't even know about 529 savings plans and that we could go on a trip just for paying tuition. Machu Picchu sounds amazing and I am glad that we get to go with Paul and Anna. I think that it will be a lot of fun."

They arrived at the assembly at 6:47 p.m. They picked up a program and found that the assembly was a graduation for Christian J. Howards. Both Allison and Justin knew the name, as he was well-known in the community for philanthropy. They entered the assembly hall and found Professor Christensen seated on the stage dressed in graduation robes.

Allison gasped with enthusiastic disbelief. "No way!" Do you really think Professor Christensen is… Christian Howards?"

Justin smiled as they took their seats. "Things are not always as they seem," he said, realizing what the professor meant from the first day of class.

At the appropriate time, the President of Syracuse State University announced that they were having a special graduation ceremony for a guest of honor. "We are pleased to announce that Christian J. Howards is being awarded an honorary doctorate degree in business administration and another honorary doctorate degree in entrepreneurism."

The president went on to describe that Christian J. Howards was the fifth of seven children. He had grown up in a rural town and later married Laura Osborn, the daughter of Gordon and Betty Osborn.

At the mention of the names of Laura Osborn's parents, both Allison and Justin had surprised looks on their faces. Justin had won the Gordon and Betty Osborn Scholarship, one of the most prestigious scholarships offered on the campus. *They were Professor Christensen's, or should he say: Professor Howard's wife's parents!*

"Christian J. Howards," continued the president, interrupting Justin's thoughts, "has given more than 50 million dollars to the university both privately and for scholarships. With a distinguished career in real estate and business leadership, Christian has founded over 20 successful businesses that benefit both local and national communities. The university wanted to honor Mr. Howards with these honorary degrees five months ago, but he refused until we let him teach a class at the university. From what I understand, many of those class members are here tonight."

Justin smiled. He realized they had been learning from a multi-millionaire without knowing it.

The degrees and accompanying awards were presented to Professor Howards. The audience applauded. The newly doctorate-awarded Professor Howards gave a brief speech about the importance of giving back to the community and also the importance of choosing to mentor other people.

He then said, "There would be no Christian J. Howards honored tonight if it were not for my wife, Laura Howards." He thanked his wife and then said to the audience, "She has been the one behind the scenes, always there, cheering and supporting, believing in me when I didn't believe in myself. I think that she deserves applause."

Professor Howards began to clap, and the audience joined in. Laura Howards looked a little sheepish at the unexpected recognition. When the applause faded, Professor Howards said, "That isn't all." He gave a cue, and someone from offstage brought a large bouquet of flowers, roses and calla lilies, in a glass vase, and presented them to his wife.

"This, my dear," said Professor Howards "is for all the times that you've supported me and were content with just helping our family and me to succeed. Thank you. Thank you for believing in me when few did." The audience cheered again, wildly. The president concluded the ceremony and dismissed the audience.

After the ceremony, Allison and Justin went up to Professor Howards who congratulated them both. "Well done," he said. "If things continue as they are, you should be well on your way to having freedom. Allison, I am so glad that you and Justin are dating, but you by yourself have done wonders. You are also on your way to becoming very rich."

"We had no idea you were Christian Howards," said Justin, "if we had known, we would have taken you more seriously. I'm sure most people would have."

"That is exactly why I didn't tell who I was. If people aren't willing to follow correct principles in a classroom, it may not matter—regardless of who teaches them. Also, I didn't want the media following me around. I will tell you, Justin and Allison, that being rich is a way to improve the world. The richer you get the more good you can do; it is both a responsibility and a privilege. You can do more to help local, national, and global economies by being rich, *and* you can have both money and freedom rewarded to you."

Justin desperately wanted to know if Professor Howards had helped Justin get the Gordon and Betty Osborn Scholarship at the beginning of the semester. He thought it might be impolite, but his curiosity was getting the better of him. "Professor, did you have anything to do with me getting a scholarship at the beginning of the semester?"

Professor Howards looked as if he were trying to not crack a smile. "You're the one who deserves any credit for the scholarships you earned," the professor replied.

Allison asked Professor Howards, "Why did you pretend to be such a jerk at the beginning of class?"

Professor Howard shrugged and said, "To get rid of people who wanted to coast. I hope you enjoyed the class."

"I've learned more than business lessons, I've learned money management, 529 savings plans, scholarships, and so much more. Thank you, Professor." Allison said.

"Also, you helped fulfill a dream of mine," Justin said. "We're going, with another couple, to Machu Picchu by paying tuition with a rewards credit card. Thank you for teaching us to aim for our goals and teaching us how to achieve them."

Professor Howard smiled and then handed them each a sealed envelope with their names on the outsides and said, "Promise me you will not open these till tomorrow."

"We promise!" Allison and Justin said in unison.

"But, what is it?" Justin asked.

"This is just a *thank you* for letting me be a part of your lives," said Professor Howards.

"Well, thank you," said Justin, and with that, they shook hands and separated.

The next morning, Allison and Justin were running together. They had put their businesses in the hands of others. All the teams agreed that it would be nice to continue to go running, but on an individual basis; Justin and Allison met up. At the end of the run they opened their envelopes from Professor Howards. The envelopes contained personalized letters thanking them for coming to the ceremony and for being a part of the class—and a check for $500!

Part of Professor Howards' letter is written below:

This $500 is to be spent on someone who needs it, anonymously; you don't have to tell anyone and no one will follow up on you. Remember, it is what you keep and what you give away that matters. Keep yourself happy by giving to others in need.

Thanks for being in the class.

—Christian Howards

Epilogue

Justin realized his three goals: he bought his property, went to Machu Picchu, and graduated free of credit card and student loans. Paul, Anna, Allison, and Justin had a fantastic time in Machu Picchu—at a low cost. The girls shared a room and the guys stayed in another. Between all the hiking and good local food, the trip was definitely memorable and a highlight for all of them. Justin donated the $500, which Professor Howards had given him to the scholarship fund; the school's donors matched student contributions. Justin's business he made with his friend Paul remained profitable. (For more information see *Winning the Money Game in College: Business*.) Justin and Allison continued to date until February, when he proposed on Valentine's Day. They were married in June of that year. Allison had bought her own property and had her own business. Their 529 savings plans helped them to both save money on school expenses and purchase properties; they got a tax discount, saved money, and invested in real estate. (For information on how he got his property, see *Winning the Money Game in College: Real Estate*.)

Paul had joined up with Justin on creating a business. Professor Howards had helped him get one elective credit. Justin and Paul continued their business. After some time, the conditions in the market changed and Justin and Paul decided that it was best to hire a group of managers run their company. Paul proposed to Anna at Christmas of that year. Their wedding was in May.

Tyler and Ashley dated for three months, but decided that things weren't working as they expected and went their separate ways. Tyler did not purchase a property until two years later: he had too much personal debt. Ashley kept her business going.

Malcolm had to learn some hard lessons (to understand why, see *Winning the Money Game in College: Business*); Dan Frederickson, Malcolm's father made sure of it. Malcolm later earned a law degree and became a lawyer like his father.

Justin's mom and dad "came out on top" largely due to having an emergency fund set aside and drastically cutting their expenses. Justin's dad found another job at a company that was more financially secure; it was good that he made the change because seven months after Justin's dad left his old company, the company went bankrupt— too much bad debt. Justin taught his parents many of the things he had learned about money and automatic success.

Justin's cousin Dave and his wife Susan eventually had to declare bankruptcy. They just couldn't keep spending on debt that they never kept in balance. Both were surprised to learn that even though they declared bankruptcy, their student loans still had to be paid. Dave later landed a job as a middle level manager with a smaller company. He worked long hours and was consistently trying to catch up by buying things when he didn't have money. He admired Justin for having the wherewithal to buy properties and start a business, and wondered how come Justin was able to have so much time and fun, while he had to work so hard to make ends meet. However, to Dave and Susan's credit, they did follow many of the principles in <u>Setting Yourself Up to Win</u> and they never again had to face bankruptcy. They had three children.

Justin first learned to focus on finances and then he had time for all the fun he wanted. He did follow Dave's advice about taking some fun classes, and took swing dance and bowling classes with Allison. Professor Howards was right: it really was just the difference that comes of simple things done slightly different. Justin and Allison continued to buy properties and run their businesses. When Justin reached the end of his four years at college, they found a larger property in foreclosure, and they decided to buy it. They found a professional management company to manage the property. After all expenses were paid, (mortgage, property management, repairs allowance, insurance, taxes, etc.) Justin and Allison netted $3,600 a month in profits for the spring and fall semesters, and $1,700 in the summer months. Justin began to invest in other properties. At the end of his college career, Justin was independently wealthy *and* had time to enjoy his life—thanks largely to what he had learned from Christian Howards.

Christian and Laura Howards went on to mentor others. Often, they were paid thousands of dollars per person to do it. They came to Justin and Allison's wedding reception in June. In the wedding guestbook, Professor Howards wrote, "Remember, Justin and Allison, it is what you choose to keep and what you choose to give away that matters. Keep each other happy and give away your hearts to each other."

The End

If you liked this book, consider:

- Going to *www.CollegeCashChampion.com*
    - Apply for scholarships that are both project and merit based scholarships (See next page for a more complete description.)

    - Watch videos to help you succeed (more concepts are taught)

    - Purchase other books by the author.

    - Referring people you know. (You will get several bonuses to save you time and money and becoming a College Cash Champion.)

- Reading *Winning the Money Game in College: Business.*
- Reading *Winning the Money Game in College: Real Estate.*
- Finding ways that you can give back to others – both by service and donations.

Opportunities for Scholarships

In writing a book on paying for college, I wanted to create different scholarships as a way of giving back. Please go to this URL http://collegecashchampion.com/scholarships/ to see scholarships. Check back periodically as different types of scholarships will arise at different points of time and different seasons.

Depending on when you visit the site, there may be both project-based scholarships (do the project and get a scholarship; I will try to make these scholarships GPA independent) and merit-based scholarships (these will require certain conditions to be met and will have minimum GPA requirements). You are welcome to apply for both. You will need to meet the requirements to be considered.

Opportunities for Fundraisers

Also, if your school, school club, or educationally-based group is looking for a fund raiser, please visit the following URL http://collegecashchampion.com/fundraising/ and look for ways to raise money for your educationally-based organization. There are some requirements that must be met, and organizations must be approved, but this is a great way to raise money that will help to support educational causes by College Cash Champion donating to your approved group.

Thank You and Acknowledgements

A special thank you is offered for everyone who has helped with this project. John Donne said "No man is an island" and that can be said of this book; the book would not be as successful as it is and has been without each of you. I greatly appreciate your help, support, and feedback to make this book better than what it was. Many of you have lived the principles taught in this book and hope that you find continued success.

Editing and Proofing:	Emily Grover, Marcia Westmoreland, Christy Ray, and Jana Roberts.
Storyline Suggestions:	Keaton Butler, Tim Johnson, Jana Roberts, Brandon Schembri, and Justin Swalberg,
Typesetting and Layout:	Daria Lacy
Cover Design:	Astrid Gay and Steven Roberts
Some of the Book Reviewers:	John Paul Brantly, Charles Dobens, Shauna Edson, Emily Grover, Tim Johnson, Christina Loud, Tiffany MarvinCarr, Nkenna Onwuzuruoha, Lauren Popp,
	Paul Ray, Christy Ray, Ashley Rees, Jana Roberts, Brandon Schembri, Justin Swalberg, and Marcia Westmoreland, and the many unnamed people at the SLCC Writing Center.
Website:	Bill Kimbley

A special thank you is also reserved for the sites that provided me with images. Thank you for allowing me to use your images to enhance the book.

Cover Images:	FreeDigitalPhotos.net	www.freedigitalphotos.net
Interior Images:	Openclipart.org	http://openclipart.org

Bibliography and Recommended Book List

The Holy Bible, King James Version. Originally published 1611.

Bach, David. *Debt Free for Life: The Finish Rich Plan for Financial Freedom.* New York: Crown Business, 2010.

Canfield, Jack. *Maximum Confidence [10 Steps to Extreme Self-Esteem] (Audio CD).* Niles, IL: Nightingale Conant, 2002.

Carnegie, Dale. *How to Win Friends & Influence People.* New York: Pocket Books, 1998.

Eker, T. Harv. *Secrets of the Millionaire Mind: Mastering the Inner Game of Wealth.* New York: HarperCollins Publishers, 2005.

Hansen, Mark Victor, and Robert G. Allen. *The One Minute Millionaire: The Enlightened Way to Wealth.* New York: Three Rivers Press, 2009.

Hill, Napoleon, and Stone, W. Clement. *Success Through a Positive Mental Attitude (2008, CD, Unabridged).* New York, NY: Simon & Schuster, 2007.

Hill, Napoleon. *Think and Grow Rich.* Radford, VA: Wilder Publications, 2007.

Olson, Jeff. *The Slight Edge: Secret to a Successful Life.* Lake Dallas, TX: Momentum Media, 2005.

Patterson, Kerry. *Influencer: The Power to Change Anything.* New York: McGraw-Hill, 2008.

Tracy, Brian. *Flight Plan How to Achieve More, Faster Than You Ever Dreamed Possible.* San Francisco, Calif: Berrett-Koehler Publishers, 2008.

Disclaimers

This is a fictional publication. Any likeness to actual persons – living or dead, organizations, or actual events is coincidental or used as fiction. Any mention company or organizational names or insignia is used to tell a story and should not be considered representing any organization.

This publication shares the ideas, opinions, suggestions, and beliefs of the author at the time of writing. The information is conveyed under the understanding that the author, publisher, and any associates are NOT offering any form of legal, tax, accounting, investing, or financial advice. If these professional services are needed, the reader is strongly encouraged to seek the advice of a competent professional, who is certified and accredited in those respective areas. The author, publisher, successors, and associates specifically disclaim any and all responsibility for liabilities, loss, injury, or risk – both personally and professionally, which may be or is incurred as either a direct or indirect consequence of the use or application of the information contained in this publication. No guarantee or warranty is expressed or implied about the accuracy of the information herein. No person or entity shall be entitled to a claim for "detrimental reliance" based on the information in this publication, and no contracting relationship is established by use of this information. No guarantee of being able to graduate from a higher learning institution is offered.

All terms, companies, trademarks, slogans, references, and other registered insignia mentioned in this publication known or suspected of being trademarks or other registered designations, have been appropriately capitalized with a "best effort attempt." Neither the publisher nor the author can attest to the accuracy of this information or the accurate use of terms. Use of any term or name in this publication should not be regarded as representing any company, organization, or product; any use of any term should not be regarded as affecting the validity of any registered marking or designation. Any mistakes in typing, wording, spelling, capitalization and the like shall in NO way be considered any form of defamation of any entity or person.

The author and/or publisher may have agreements made with third parties mentioned in this publication wherein compensation of some sort may be offered to either the author or publisher – separately or jointly. For the vast majority of organizations and services mentioned in this publication, no agreement of compensation has been made; however, that does not preclude future agreements that can be made before and after releasing this publication. If in doubt, it is best to assume that there is an agreement of compensation, and all advice shall be considered as that of a compensated relationship for promotion, gain, and benefit. No party shall be liable for the actions or inactions of its partners or affiliates. Any opinions, advice, statements, services, offers, suggestions, ideas, or other informational content by third parties are those of the author or publisher and shall not be considered binding upon any party. The views expressed in this publication do NOT represent the opinions, beliefs, statements, or offers of any other person or organization.

The use of terms that are religious in nature are not offered with the intent of representing any specific religion or sect. All religious terms are considered for story-telling purposes and not to be ascribed as referring to or embracing any particular religious sect. While the author and publisher have made the attempt to make it non-denominational, this does not guarantee that any view or interpretation is in accordance with any religious sect. No attempt is made to convert any person to any belief, and neither defamation nor distortion of beliefs is intended.

If this has come as an ebook, then it is licensed for the original purchaser (one person). This book, as an ebook, may not be resold, redistributed, given away, duplicated, posted online, or transferred in whole or in part to another person or entity. Please purchase an additional license or copy for each person, without sharing copies. Any form of piracy is illegal, and any reproduction or distribution without consent from the publisher subjects any individual violating these terms to criminal prosecution. If you are reading this book and are not the original purchaser or original intended recipient, you should return it and purchase your own copy.

About the Author

Steven Roberts graduated from Brigham Young University in December 2008. Steven received 11 scholarships and grants during his undergraduate degree – allowing him to earn more money than what tuition and books cost him. About his books, Steven said: "I was not a perfect student, but if I had known then what I know from writing this book about paying for college, I would have saved even more on college and would have been better prepared financially."

Steven lives near Ogden, UT and has a wonderful wife and daughter – and a son on the way. Steven enjoys hiking, cooking, writing, and spending time with his wife and family. Steven is also passionate about saving money and having fun. His goal is to help raise $10 million dollars for educational causes and charities.

Steven would enjoy hearing from his readers. To contact him about his books, schedule a speaking engagement for him to speak at, book signings, or to share your successes please email Steven at:

Steven.Roberts.1@CollegeCashChampion.com

Note: Orders and shipping questions should go to:

Orders@CollegeCashChampion.com

Please be courteous and send the information to the appropriate destination.

Quick Order Form

Web (easiest and fasted method to order):

www.CollegeCashChampion.com

Email:

Orders@CollegeCashChampion.com

Postal Orders:

College Cash Champion, Steven Roberts
98 N Main Street #222, Clearfield, UT 84015

Please send the following items (and quantities):

_____

_____

_____

Please send more FREE information on:

☐ Other Books   ☐ Book Signings   ☐ Video Courses
☐ Seminars   ☐ Speaking Engagements

Name: _____

Address: _____

City: _____ State: _____ Zip: _____

Telephone: _____

Email: _____

Sales Tax: Please add 7% to any order shipped in Utah.

U.S. Shipping: $5.75 for the first physical book, $3.00 for every item thereafter. For orders over 10 items, please email or visit the website or email. Payment is due before items are sent out. Thanks.